I

1

Barbara wished she would come back. For the last hour Fanny Waddington had kept on passing in and out of the room through the open door into the garden, bringing in tulips, white, pink, and red tulips, for the flowered Lowestoft bowls, hovering over them, caressing them with her delicate butterfly fingers, humming some sort of song to herself.

The song mixes itself up with the Stores list Barbara was making: "Two dozen glass towels. Twelve pounds of Spratt's puppy biscuits. One dozen gent.'s all-silk pyjamas, extra large size" ... "A-hoom—hoom, a-hoom—hoom" (that *Impromptu* of Schubert's), and with the notes Barbara was writing: "Mrs. Waddington has pleasure in enclosing...." Fanny Waddington would always have pleasure in enclosing something.... "A ho-om—boom, hoom, hee." A sound so light that it hardly stirred the quiet of the room. If a butterfly could hum it would hum like Fanny Waddington.

Barbara Madden had not been two days at Lower Wyck Manor, and already she was at home there; she knew by heart Fanny's drawing-room with the low stretch of the Tudor windows at each end, their lattices panelled by the heavy mullions, the back one looking out on to the green garden bordered with wallflowers and tulips; the front one on to the round grass-plot and the sundial, the drive and the shrubbery beyond, down the broad walk that cut through it into the clear reaches of the park. She liked the interior, the Persian carpet faded to patches of grey and fawn and old rose, the port-wine mahogany furniture, the tables thrusting out the brass claws of their legs, the latticed cabinets and bookcases, the chintz curtains and chair-covers, all red dahlias and powder-blue parrots on a cream-coloured ground. But when Fanny wasn't there you could feel the room ache with the emptiness she left.

Barbara ached. She caught herself listening for Fanny Waddington's feet on the flagged path and the sound of her humming. As she waited she looked up at the picture over the bureau in the recess of the fireplace, the portrait in oils of Horatio Bysshe Waddington, Fanny's husband.

He was seated, heavily seated with his spread width and folded height, in one of the brown-leather chairs of his library, dressed in a tweed coat, putty-coloured riding breeches, a buff waistcoat, and a grey-blue tie. The handsome, florid face was lifted in a noble pose above the stiff white collar; you could see the full, slightly drooping lower lip under the shaggy black moustache. There was solemnity in the thick, rounded salient of the Roman nose, in the slightly bulging eyes, and in the almost imperceptible line that sagged from each nostril down the long curve of the cheeks. This figure, one great thigh crossed on the other, was extraordinarily solid against the smoky background where the clipped black hair made a watery light. His eyes were not looking at anything in particular. Horatio Bysshe Waddington seemed to be absorbed in some solemn thought.

His wife's portrait hung over the card-table in the other recess.

Barbara hoped he would be nice; she hoped he would be interesting, since she had to be his secretary. But, of course, he would be. Anybody so enchanting as Fanny could never have married him if he wasn't. She wondered how she, Barbara Madden, would play her double part of secretary to him and companion to her. She had been secretary to other men before; all through the war she had been secretary to somebody, but she had never had to be companion to their wives. Perhaps it was a good thing that Fanny, as she kept on reminding her, had "secured" her first. She was glad he wasn't there when she arrived and wouldn't be till the day after to-morrow (he had wired that morning to tell them); so that for two days more she would have Fanny to herself.

2

"Well, what do you think of him?"

Fanny had come back into the room; she was hovering behind her.

"I—I think he's jolly good-looking."

"Well, you see, that was painted seventeen years ago. He was young then."

"Has he changed much since?"

"Dear me, no," said Fanny. "He hasn't changed at all."

"No more have you, I think."

"Oh, *me*—in seventeen years!"

She was still absurdly like her portrait, after seventeen years, with her light, slender body, poised for one of her flights, her quick movements of butterfly and bird, with her small white face, the terrier nose lifted on the moth-wing shadows of her nostrils, her dark-blue eyes, that gazed at you, close under the low black eyebrows, her brown hair that sprang in two sickles from the peak on her forehead, raking up to the backward curve of the chignon, a profile of cyclamen. And her mouth, the fine lips drawn finer by her enchanting smile. All these features set in such strange, sensitive unity that her mouth looked at you and her eyes said things. No matter how long she lived she would always be young.

"Oh, my dear child," she said, "you are so like your mother."

Mr. Waddington of Wyck

May Sinclair

Alpha Editions

This edition published in 2023

ISBN : 9789357953948

Design and Setting By
Alpha Editions
www.alphaedis.com
Email - info@alphaedis.com

Contents

"Am I? Were you afraid I wouldn't be?"

"A little, just a little afraid. I thought you'd be modern."

"So I am. So was mother."

"Not when I knew her."

"Afterwards then." A sudden thought came to Barbara. "Mrs. Waddington, if mother was your dearest friend why haven't you known me all this time?"

"Your mother and I lost sight of each other before you were born."

"Mother didn't want to."

"Nor I."

"Mother would have hated you to think she did."

"I never thought it. She must have known I didn't."

"Then why—"

"Did we lose sight?"

"Yes, why? People don't, if they can help it, if they care enough. And mother cared."

"You're a persistent little thing, aren't you? Are you trying to make out that I didn't care?"

"I'm trying to make you see that mother did."

"Well, my dear, we both cared, but we *couldn't* help it. We married, and our husbands didn't hit it off."

"Didn't they? And daddy was so nice. Didn't you know how nice he was?"

"Oh, yes. I knew. My husband was nice, too, Barbara; though you mightn't think it."

"Oh, but I do. I'm sure he is. Only I haven't seen him yet."

"So nice. But," said Fanny, pursuing her own thought, "he never made a joke in his life, and your father never *made* anything else."

"Daddy didn't 'make' jokes. They came to him."

"I've seen them come. He never sent any of them away, no matter how naughty they were, or how expensive. I used to adore his jokes.... But Horatio didn't. He didn't like my adoring them, so you see—"

"I see. I wonder," said Barbara, looking up at the portrait again, "what he's thinking about?"

"I used to wonder."

"But you know now?"

"Yes, I know now," Fanny said.

"What'll happen," said Barbara, "if *I* make jokes?"

"Nothing. He'll never see them."

"If he saw daddy's—"

"Oh, but he didn't. That was me."

Barbara was thoughtful. "I daresay," she said, "you won't keep me long. Supposing I can't do the work?"

"The *work*?" Fanny's eyes were interrogative and a little surprised, as though they were saying, "Who said work? What work?"

"Well, Mr. Waddington's work. I've got to help him with his book, haven't I?"

"Oh, his book, yes. *When* he's writing it. He isn't always. Does he look," said Fanny, "like a man who'd always be writing a book?"

"No. I can't say he does, exactly." (What *did* he look like?)

"Well, then, it'll be all right. I mean *we* shall be."

"I only wondered whether I could really do what he wants."

"If Ralph could," said Fanny, "you can."

"Who's Ralph?"

"Ralph is my cousin. He *was* Horatio's secretary."

"*Was*." Barbara considered it. "Did *he* make jokes, then?"

"Lots. But that wasn't why he left…. It was an awful pity, too; because he's most dreadfully hard up."

"If he's hard up," Barbara said, "I couldn't bear to think I've done him out of a job."

"You haven't. He had to go."

Fanny turned again to her flowers and Barbara to her Stores list.

"Are you sure," Fanny said suddenly, "you put 'striped'?"

"Striped? The pyjamas? No, I haven't."

"Then, for goodness' sake, put it. Supposing they sent those awful Futurist things; why, he'd frighten me into fits. Can't you see Horatio stalking in out of his dressing-room, all magenta blobs and forked lightning?"

"I haven't seen him at all yet," said Barbara.

"Well, you wait.... Does my humming annoy you?"

"Not a bit. I like it. It's such a happy sound."

"I always do it," said Fanny, "when I'm happy."

You could hear feet, feet in heavy soled boots, clanking on the drive that ringed the grass-plot and the sundial; the eager feet of a young man. Fanny turned her head, listening.

"There *is* Ralph," she said. "Come in, Ralph!"

The young man stood in the low, narrow doorway, filling it with his slender height and breadth. He looked past Fanny, warily, into the far corner of the room, and when his eyes found Barbara at her bureau they smiled.

"Oh, *come* in," Fanny said. "He isn't here. He won't be till Friday. This is Ralph Bevan, Barbara; and this is Barbara Madden, Ralph."

He bowed, still smiling, as if he saw something irrepressibly amusing in her presence there.

"Yes," said Fanny to the smile. "Your successor."

"I congratulate you, Miss Madden."

"Don't be an ironical beast. She's just said she couldn't bear to think she'd done you out of your job."

"Well, I couldn't," said Barbara.

"That's very nice of you. But you didn't do me out of anything. It was the act of God."

"It was Horatio's act. Not that Miss Madden meant any reflection on his justice and his mercy."

"I don't know about his justice," Ralph said. "But he was absolutely merciful when he fired me out."

"Is it so awfully hard then?" said Barbara.

"You may not find it so."

"Oh, but I'm going to be Mrs. Waddington's companion, too."

"You'll be all right then. They wouldn't let *me* be that."

"He means you'll be safe, dear. You won't be fired out whatever happens."

"Whatever sort of secretary I am?"

"Yes. She can be any sort she likes, in reason, can't she?"

"She can't be a worse one than I was, anyhow."

Barbara was aware that he had looked at her, a long look, half thoughtful, half amused, as if he were going to say something different, something that would give her a curious light on herself, and had thought better of it.

Fanny Waddington was protesting. "My dear boy, it wasn't for incompetence. She's simply dying to know what you *did* do."

"You can tell her."

"He wanted to write Horatio's book for him, and Horatio wouldn't let him. That was all."

"Oh, well, *I* shan't want to write it," Barbara said.

"We thought perhaps you wouldn't," said Fanny.

But Barbara had turned to her bureau, affecting a discreet absorption in her list. And presently Ralph Bevan went out into the garden with Fanny to gather more tulips.

II

1

She *had* been dying to know what he had done, but now, after Ralph had stayed to lunch and tea and dinner that first day, after he had spent all yesterday at the Manor, and after he had turned up to-day at ten o'clock in the morning, Barbara thought she had made out the history, though they had been very discreet and Fanny had insisted on reading "Tono-Bungay" out loud half the time.

Ralph, of course, was in love with his cousin Fanny. To be sure, she must be at least ten years older than he was, but that wouldn't matter. And, of course, it was rather naughty of him, but then again, very likely he couldn't help it. It had just come on him when he wasn't thinking; and who could help being in love with Fanny? You could be in love with people quite innocently and hopelessly. There was no sin where there wasn't any hope.

And perhaps Fanny was innocently, ever so innocently, in love with him; or, if she wasn't, Horatio thought she was, which came to much the same thing; so that anyhow poor Ralph had to go. The explanation they had given, Barbara thought, was rather thin, not quite worthy of their admirable intelligence.

It was Friday, Barbara's fifth day. She was walking home with Ralph Bevan through the Waddingtons' park, down the main drive that led from Wyck-on-the-Hill to Lower Wyck Manor.

It wouldn't be surprising, she thought, if Fanny were in love with her cousin; he was, as she put it to herself, so distinctly "fallable-in-love-with." She could see Fanny surrendering, first to his sudden laughter, his quick, delighted mind, his innocent, engaging frankness. He would, she thought, be endlessly amusing, endlessly interesting, because he was so interested, so amused. There was something that pleased her in the way he walked, hatless, his head thrown back, his shoulders squared, his hands thrust into his coat pockets, safe from gesture; something in the way he spun round in his path to face her with his laughter. He had Fanny's terrier nose with the ghost of a kink in it; his dark hair grew back in a sickle on each temple; it wouldn't lie level and smooth like other people's, but sprang up, curled from the clipping. His eyes were his own, dappled eyes, green and grey, black and brown, sparkling; so was his mouth, which was neither too thin nor too thick—determination in the thrusting curve of that lower lip—and his chin, which was just a shade too big for it, a shade too big for his face. His cheeks were sunburnt, and a little shower of ochreish freckles spread from the sunburn and peppered the slopes of his nose. She wanted to sketch him.

"Doesn't Mrs. Waddington ever go for walks?" she said.

"Fanny? No. She's too lazy."

"Lazy?"

"Too active, if you like, in other ways…. How long have you known her?"

"Just five days."

"Five *days*?"

"Yes; but, you see, years ago she was my mother's dearest friend. That's how I came to be their secretary. When she saw my name in the advertisement she thought it must be me. And it was me. They hadn't seen each other for years and years. My father and Mr. Waddington didn't hit it off together, I believe."

"You haven't seen him yet?"

"No. There seems to be some mystery about him."

"Mystery?"

"Yes. What is it? Or mayn't you tell?"

"I *won't* tell. It wouldn't be kind."

"Then don't—don't. I didn't know it was that sort of thing."

Ralph laughed. "It isn't. I meant it wouldn't be kind to you. I don't want to spoil him for you."

"Then there *is*—tell me one thing: Shall I get on with him all right?"

"Don't ask me *that*."

"I mean, will he be awfully difficult to work with?"

"Because he sacked me? No. Only you mustn't let on that you know better than he does. And if you want to keep your job, you mustn't contradict him."

"Now you've made me want to contradict him. Whatever he says I shall have to say the other thing whether I agree with him or not."

"Don't you think you could temporize a bit? For her sake."

"Did *you* temporize?"

"Rather. I was as meek and servile as I knew how."

"As you knew how. Do you think I shall know better?"

"Yes, you're a woman. You can get on the right side of him. Will you try to, because of Fanny? I'm most awfully glad she's got you, and I want you to stay. Between you and me she has a very thin time with Waddington."

"There it is. I know—I know—I *know* I'm going to hate him."

"Oh, no, you're not. You can't *hate* Waddington."

"*You* don't?"

"Oh, Lord, no. I wouldn't mind him a bit, poor old thing, if he wasn't Fanny's husband."

He had almost as good as owned it, almost put her in possession of their secret. She conceived it—his secret, Fanny's secret—as all innocence on her part, all chivalry on his; tender and hopeless and pure.

2

They had come to the white gate that led between the shrubberies and the grass-plot with the yellow-grey stone house behind it.

It was nice, she thought, of Fanny to make Mr. Bevan take her for these long walks when she couldn't go with them; but Barbara felt all the time that she ought to apologize to the young man for not being Fanny, especially when Mr. Waddington was coming back to-day by the three-forty train and this afternoon would be their last for goodness knew how long. And as they talked—about Ralph's life before the war and the jobs he had lost because of it (he had been a journalist), and about Barbara's job at the War Office, and air raids and the games they both went in for, and their favourite authors and the room he had in the White Hart Inn at Wyck—as they talked, fluently, with the ease of old acquaintances, almost of old friends, Barbara admired the beauty of Mr. Bevan's manners; you would have supposed that instead of suffering, as he must be suffering, agonies of impatience and irritation, he had never enjoyed anything in his life so much as this adventure that was just coming to an end.

He had opened the gate for her and now stood with his back to it, holding out his hand, saying "Good-bye."

"Aren't you coming in?" she said. "Mrs. Waddington expects you for tea."

"No," he said, "she doesn't. She knows I can't come if he's there."

He paused. "By the way, that book of his, it's in an appalling muddle. I hadn't time to do much to it before I left. If you can't get it straight you must come to me and I'll help you."

"That's very good of you."

"Rather not. It *was* my job, you know."

He was backing through the gate, saluting as he went. And now he had turned and was running with raking, athletic paces up the grass border of the park.

III

1

"Tea is in the library, miss."

This announcement, together with Partridge's extraordinary increase of importance, would have told her that the master had returned, even if she had not seen, through the half-open door of the cloak-room, Mr. Waddington's overcoat hanging by its shoulders and surmounted by his grey slouch hat.

With a rapid, furtive movement the butler closed the door on these sanctities; and she noted the subdued quiet of his footsteps as he led the way down the dark oak-panelled corridor, through the smoke-room, and into the library beyond. She also caught a surprising sight of her own face in the glass over the smoke-room chimneypiece, her dark eyes shining, the cool, wind-beaten flush on her young cheeks, the curled mouth flowering, geranium red on rose white.

This Barbara of the looking-glass smiled at her in passing with such gay, irresponsible amusement that it fairly took her breath away. Its origin became clear to her as Ralph Bevan's words shot into her mind: "I don't want to spoil him for you." She foresaw a possible intimacy in which Horatio Bysshe Waddington would become the unique though unofficial tie between them. She was aware that it pleased her to share a secret jest with Ralph Bevan.

She found Fanny established behind her tea-table in the low room, dim with its oak panelling above the long lines of the bookcases, where Fanny's fluttering smile made movement and a sort of light.

Her husband sat facing her in his brown leather chair and in the pose, the wonderful pose of his portrait; only the sobriety of his navy-blue serge had fined it down, giving him a factitious slenderness. He hadn't seen her come in. He sat there in innocence and unawareness; and afterwards it gave her a little pang of remorse remembering how innocent he had then seemed to her and unaware.

"This is my husband, Barbara. Horatio, you haven't met Miss Madden."

His eyes bulged with the startled innocence of a creature taken unaware. He had just lifted his face, with its dripping moustache, from his teacup, and though he carried off this awkwardness with an unabashed sweep of his pocket-handkerchief, you could see that he was sensitive; he hated you to catch him in any gesture that was less than noble. All his gestures were noble and his attitudes. He was noble as he got up, slowly, unfolding his great height, tightening by a movement of his shoulders his great breadth. He looked down at her superbly and held out his hand; it closed on hers in a large genial clasp.

"So this is my secretary, is it?"

"Yes. And don't forget she's my companion as well as your secretary."

"I never forget anything that you wish me to remember." (Only he said "nevah" and "remembah"; he bowed as he said it in a very courtly way.)

Barbara noticed that his black hair and moustache were lightly grizzled, there was loose flesh about his eyelids, his chin had doubled, and his cheeks were sagging from the bone, otherwise he was exactly like his portrait; these changes made him look, if anything, more incorruptibly dignified and more solemn. He had remained on his feet (for his breeding was perfect), moving between the tea-table and Barbara, bringing her tea, milk and sugar, and things to eat. Altogether he was so simple, so genial and unmysterious that Barbara could only suppose that Ralph had been making fun of her, of her wonder, her curiosity.

"My dear, what a colour you've got!"

Fanny put up her hands to her own cheeks to draw attention to Barbara's. "You *are* growing a country girl, aren't you? You should have seen her white face when she came, Horatio."

"What has she been doing to herself?" He had settled again into his chair and his attitude.

"She's been out walking with Ralph."

"With Ralph? Is *he* here still?"

"Why shouldn't he be?"

Mr. Waddington shrugged his immense shoulders. "It's a question of taste. If he *likes* to hang about the place after his behaviour—"

"Poor boy! whatever has he done? 'Behaviour' makes it sound as if it had been something awful."

"We needn't go into it, I think."

"But you *are* going into it, darling, all the time. Do you mean to keep it up against him for ever?"

"I'm not keeping anything up. What Ralph Bevan does is no concern of mine. Since I'm not to be inconvenienced by it—since Miss Madden has come to my rescue so charmingly—I shall not give it another thought."

He turned to Barbara as to a change of subject. "Had you any difficulty"—
(his voice was measured and important)—"in finding your way here?"

"None at all."

"Ah, that one-thirty train is excellent. Excellent. But if you had not told the
guard to stop at the Hill you would have been carried on to Cheltenham.
Which would have been very awkward for you. Very awkward indeed."

"My dear Horatio, what did you suppose she *would* do?"

"My dear Fanny, there are many things she might have done. She might have
got into the wrong coach at Paddington and been carried on to Worcester."

"And that," said Barbara, "would have been much worse than Cheltenham."

"The very thought of it," said Fanny, "makes me shudder. But thank God,
Barbara, you didn't do any of those things."

Mr. Waddington shifted the crossing of his legs as a big dog shifts his paws
when you laugh at him; the more Fanny laughed the more dignified and
solemn he became.

"You haven't told me yet, Horatio, what you did in London."

"I was just going to tell you when Miss Madden—so delightfully—came in."

At that Barbara thought it discreet to dismiss herself, but Fanny called her
back. "What are you running away for? He didn't do anything in London he
wouldn't like you to hear about."

"On the contrary, I particularly wish Miss Madden to hear about it. I am
starting a branch of the National League of Liberty in Wyck. You may have
heard of it?"

"Yes. I've *heard* of it. I've even seen the prospectus."

"Good. Well, Fanny, I lunched yesterday with Sir Maurice Gedge, and he's
as keen as mustard. He agrees with me that the League will be no good, no
good at all, until it's taken up strong in the provinces. He wants me to start
at once. Just as soon as I can get my Committee."

"My dear, if you've got to have a Committee first you'll never start."

"It depends altogether on who I get. And it'll be *my* Committee. Sir Maurice
was very emphatic about that. He agrees with me that if you want a thing
done, and done well, you must do it yourself. There can only be *one* moving
spirit. The Committee will have nothing to do but carry out my ideas."

"Then be sure you get a Committee that hasn't any of its own."

"That will not be difficult," said Mr. Waddington, "in Wyck.... The first thing is the prospectus. That's where you come in, Miss Madden."

"You mean the first thing is that Barbara draws up the prospectus."

"Under my supervision."

"The next thing," Fanny said, "is to conceal your prospectus from your Committee till it's in print. You come to your Committee with your prospectus. You don't offer it for discussion."

"Supposing," Barbara said, "they insist on discussing it?"

"They won't," said Fanny, "once it's printed, especially if it's paid for. You must get Pyecraft to send in his bill at once. And if they *do* start discussing you can put them off with the date and place of the meeting and the wording of the posters. That'll give them something to talk about. I suppose you'll be chairman."

"Well, I think, in the circumstances, they could hardly appoint anybody else."

"I don't know. Somebody might suggest Sir John Corbett."

Mr. Waddington's face sagged with dismay as Fanny presented this unpleasant possibility.

"I don't think Sir John would care about it. I shall suggest it to him myself; but I don't think—."

After all, Sir John Corbett was a lazy man.

"When you've roused Sir John, if you ever *do* rouse him, then you'll have to round up all the towns and villages for twenty miles. It's a pity you can't have Ralph; he would have rounded them for you in no time on his motor-bike."

"I am quite capable of rounding them all up myself, thank you."

"Well, dear," said Fanny placably, "it'll keep you busy for the next six months, and that'll be nice. You won't miss the war then so much, will you?"

"*Miss the war?*"

"Yes, you do miss it, darling. He was a special constable, Barbara; and he sat on tribunals; and he drove his motor-car like mad on government service. He had no end of a time. It's no use your saying you didn't enjoy it, Horatio, for you did."

"I was glad to be of service to my country as much as any soldier, but to say that I enjoyed the war—"

"If there hadn't been a war there wouldn't have been any service to be glad about."

"My dear Fanny, it's a perfectly horrible suggestion. Do you mean to say that I would have brought about that—that infamous tragedy, that I would have sent thousands and thousands of our lads to their deaths to get a job for myself? If I thought for one moment that you were serious—"

"You don't like me to be anything else, dear."

"I certainly don't like you to joke about such subjects."

"Oh, come," said Fanny, "we all enjoyed our war jobs except poor Ralph, who got gassed first thing, and *then* concussed with a shell-burst."

"Oh, did he?" said Barbara.

"He did. And don't you think, Horatio, considering the rotten time he's had, and that he lost a lucrative job through the war, and that you've done him out of his secretaryship, don't you think you might forgive him?"

"Of course," said Horatio, "I forgive him."

He had got up to go and had reached the door when Fanny called him back. "And I can write and ask him to come and dine to-morrow night, can't I? I want to be quite sure that he *does* dine."

"I have never said or implied," said Horatio, "that he was not to come and dine."

With that he left them.

"The beautiful thing about Horatio," said Fanny, "is that he never bears a grudge against people, no matter what he's done to them. I've no doubt that Ralph was excessively provoking and put him in the wrong, and yet, though he was in the wrong, and knows he was in it, he doesn't resent it. He doesn't resent it the least little bit."

2

Barbara wondered how and where she would be expected to spend her evenings now that Fanny's husband had come home. Being secretary to Mr. Waddington and companion to Fanny wouldn't mean being companion to both of them at once. So when Horatio appeared in the drawing-room after coffee, she asked if she might sit in the morning-room and write letters.

"Do you want to sit in the morning-room?" said Fanny.

"Well, I ought to write those letters."

"There's a fire in the library. You can write there. Can't she, Horatio?"

Mr. Waddington looked up with the benign expression he had had when he came on Barbara alone in the drawing-room before dinner, a look so directed to her neck and shoulders that it told her how well her low-cut evening frock became her.

"She shall sit anywhere she likes. The library is hers whenever she wants to use it."

Barbara thought she would rather like the library. As she went she couldn't help seeing a look on Fanny's face that pleaded, that would have kept her with her. She thought: She doesn't want to be alone with him.

She judged it better to ignore that look.

She had been about an hour in the library; she had written her letters and chosen a book and curled herself up in the big leather chair and was reading when Mr. Waddington came in. He took no notice of her at first, but established himself at the writing-table with his back to her. He would, of course, want her to go. She uncurled herself and went quietly to the door.

Mr. Waddington looked up.

"You needn't go," he said.

Something in his face made her wonder whether she ought to stay. She remembered that she was Mrs. Waddington's companion.

"Mrs. Waddington may want me."

"Mrs. Waddington has gone to bed…. Don't go—unless you're tired. I'm getting my thoughts on paper and I may want you."

She remembered that she was Mr. Waddington's secretary.

She went back to her chair. It was only his face that had made her wonder. His great back, bent to his task, was like another person there; absorbed and unmoved, it chaperoned them. From time to time she heard brief scratches of his pen as he got a thought down. It was ten o'clock.

When the half-hour struck Mr. Waddington gave a thick "Ha!" of irritation and got up.

"It's no use," he said. "I'm not in form to-night. I suppose it's the journey."

He came to the fireplace and sat down heavily in the opposite chair. Barbara was aware of his eyes, considering, appraising her.

"My wife tells me she has had a delightful time with you."

"I've had a delightful time with her."

"I'm glad. My wife is a very delightful woman; but, you know, you mustn't take everything she says too seriously."

"I won't. I'm not a very serious person myself."

"Don't say that. Don't say that."

"Very well. I think, if you don't want me, I'll say good night."

"Seriously?"

"Seriously."

He had risen as she rose and went to open the door for her. He escorted her through the smoke-room and stood there at the further door, holding out his hand, benignant and superbly solemn.

"Good night, then," he said.

She told herself that she was wrong, quite wrong about his poor old face. There was nothing in it, nothing but that grave and unadventurous benignity. His mood had been, she judged, purely paternal. Paternal and childlike, too; pathetic, if you came to think of it, in his clinging to her presence, her companionship. "It must have been my little evil mind," she thought.

3

As she went along the corridor she remembered she had left her knitting in the drawing-room. She turned to fetch it and found Fanny still there, wide awake with her feet on the fender, and reading "Tono-Bungay."

"Oh, Mrs. Waddington, I thought you'd gone to bed."

"So did I, dear. But I changed my mind when I found myself alone with Wells. He's too heavenly for words."

Barbara saw it in a flash, then. She knew what she, the companion and secretary, was there for. She was there to keep him off her, so that Fanny might have more time to find herself alone in.

She saw it all.

"'Tono-Bungay,'" she said. "Was *that* what you sent me out with Mr. Bevan for?"

"It was. How clever of you, Barbara."

IV

1

Mr. Waddington closed the door on Miss Madden slowly and gently so that the action should not strike her as dismissive. He then turned on the lights by the chimneypiece and stood there, looking at himself in the glass. He wanted to know exactly how his face had presented itself to Miss Madden. It would not be altogether as it appeared to himself; for the glass, unlike the young girl's clear eyes, was an exaggerating and distorting medium; he had noticed that his wife's face in the smoke-room glass looked a good ten years older than the face he knew; he calculated, therefore, that this faint greenish tint, this slightly lop-sided elderly grimace were not truthful renderings of his complexion and his smile. And as (in spite of these defects, which you could put down to the account of the glass) the face Mr. Waddington saw was still the face of a handsome man, he formed a very favourable opinion of the face Miss Madden had seen. Handsome, and if not in his first youth, then still in his second. Experience is itself a fascination, and if a man has any charm at all his second youth should be more charming, more irresistibly fascinating than his first.

And the child had been conscious of him. She had betrayed uneasiness, a sense of danger, when she had found herself alone with him. He recalled her first tentative flight, her hesitation. He would have liked to have kept her there with him a little longer, to have talked to her about his League, to have tested by a few shrewd questions her ability.

Better not. Better not. The child was wise and right. Her wisdom and rectitude were delicious to Mr. Waddington, still more so was the thought that she had felt him to be dangerous.

He went back into his library and sat again in his chair and meditated: This experiment of Fanny's now; he wondered how it would turn out, especially if Fanny really wanted to adopt the girl, Frank Madden's daughter. That impudent social comedian had been so offensive to Mr. Waddington in his life-time that there was something alluring in the idea of keeping his daughter now that he was dead, seeing the exquisite little thing dependent on him for everything, for food and frocks and pocket-money. But no doubt they had been wise in giving her the secretaryship before committing themselves to the irrecoverable step; thus testing her in a relation that could be easily terminated if by any chance it proved embarrassing.

But the relation in itself was, as Mr. Waddington put it to himself, a little difficult and delicate. It involved an intimacy, a closer intimacy than adoption:

having her there in his library at all hours to work with him; and always that little uneasy consciousness of hers.

Well, well, he had set the tone to-night for all their future intercourse; he had in the most delicate way possible let her see. It seemed to him, looking back on it, that he had exercised a perfect tact, parting from her with that air of gaiety and light badinage which his own instinct of self-preservation so happily suggested. Yet he smiled when he recalled her look as she went from him, backing, backing, to the door; it made him feel very tender and chivalrous; virtuous too, as if somehow he had overcome some unforeseen and ruinous impulse. And all the time he hadn't had any impulse beyond the craving to talk to an intelligent and attractive stranger, to talk about his League.

Mr. Waddington went to bed thinking about it. He even woke his wife up out of her sleep with the request that she would remind him to call at Underwoods first thing in the morning.

2

As soon as he was awake he thought of Underwoods. Underwoods was important. He had to round up the county, and he couldn't do that without first consulting Sir John Corbett, of Underwoods. As a matter of form, a mere matter of form, of course, he would have to consult him.

But the more he thought about it the less he liked the idea of consulting anybody. He was desperately afraid that, if he once began letting people into it, his scheme, his League, would be taken away from him; and that the proper thing, the graceful thing, the thing to which he would be impelled by all his instincts and traditions, would be to stand modestly back and see it go. Probably into Sir John Corbett's hands. And he couldn't. He couldn't. Yet it was clear that the League, just because it was a League, must have members; even if he had been prepared to contribute all the funds himself and carry on the whole business of it single-handed, it couldn't consist solely of Mr. Waddington of Wyck. His problem was a subtle and difficult one: How to identify himself with the League, himself alone, in a unique and indissoluble manner, and yet draw to it the necessary supporters? How to control every detail of its intricate working (there would be endless wheels within wheels), and at the same time give proper powers to the inevitable Committee? If he did not put it quite so crudely as Fanny in her disagreeable irony, his problem resolved itself into this: How to divide the work and yet rake in all the credit?

He was saved from its immediate pressure by the sight of the envelope that waited for him on the breakfast-table, addressed in a familiar hand.

"Mrs. Levitt——" His emotion betrayed itself to Barbara in a peculiar furtive yet triumphant smile.

"Again?" said Fanny. (There was no end to the woman and her letters.)

Mrs. Levitt requested Mr. Waddington to call on her that morning at eleven. There was a matter on which she desired to consult him. The brevity of the note revealed her trust in his compliance, trust that implied again a certain intimacy. Mr. Waddington read it out loud to show how harmless and open was his communion with Mrs. Levitt.

"Is there any matter on which she has not consulted you?"

"There seems to have been one. And, as you see, she is repairing the omission."

A light air, a light air, to carry off Mrs. Levitt. The light air that had carried off Barbara, that had made Barbara carry herself off the night before. (It had done good. This morning the young girl was all ease and innocent unconsciousness again.)

"And I suppose you're going?" Fanny said.

"I suppose I shall have to go."

"Then I shall have Barbara to myself all morning?"

"You will have Barbara to yourself all day."

He tried thus jocosely to convey, for Barbara's good, his indifference to having her. All the same, it gave him pleasure to say her name like that: "Barbara."

He was not sure that he wanted to go and see Mrs. Levitt with all this business of the League on hand. It meant putting off Sir John. You couldn't do Sir John *and* Mrs. Levitt in one morning. Besides, he thought he knew what Mrs. Levitt wanted, and he said to himself that this time he would be obliged, for once, to refuse her.

But it was not in him to refuse to go and see her. So he went.

As he walked up the park drive to the town he recalled with distinctly pleasurable emotion the first time he had encountered Mrs. Levitt, the vision of the smart little lady who had stood there by the inner gate, the gate that led from the park into the grounds, waiting for his approach with happy confidence. He remembered her smile, an affair of milk-white teeth in an ivory-white face, and her frank attack: "Forgive me if I'm trespassing. They told me there was a right of way." He remembered her charming diffidence, the naïve reverence for his "grounds" which had compelled him to escort her personally through them; her attitudes of admiration as the Manor burst on her from its bay in the beech trees; the interest she had shown in its date and architecture; and how, spinning out the agreeable interview, he had gone with her all the way to the farther gate that led into Lower Wyck village; and how she had challenged him there with her "You must be Mr. Waddington of Wyck," and capped his admission with "I'm Mrs. Levitt." To which he had replied that he was delighted.

And the time after that—Partridge had discreetly shown her into the library—when she had called to implore him to obtain exemption for her son Toby; her black eyes, bright and large behind tears; and her cry: "I'm a war widow, Mr. Waddington, and he's my only child;" the flattery of her belief that he, Mr. Waddington of Wyck, had the chief power on the tribunal (and indeed it would have been folly to pretend that he had not power, that he could not "work it" if he chose). And the third time, after he had "worked it," and she had come to thank him. Tears again; the pressure of a plump, ivory-white hand; a tingling, delicious memory.

After that, his untiring efforts to get a war job for Toby. There had been difficulties, entailing many visits to Mrs. Levitt in the little house in the Market Square of Wyck-on-the-Hill; but in the end he had had the same intoxicating experience of his power, all obstructions going down before Mr. Waddington of Wyck.

And this year, when Toby was finally demobilized, it was only natural that she should draw on Mr. Waddington's influence again to get him a permanent peace job. He had got it; and that meant more visits and more gratitude; till here he was, attached to Mrs. Levitt by the unbreakable tie of his benefactions. He was even attached to her son Toby, whose continued existence, to say nothing of his activity in Mr. Bostock's Bank at Wyck, was a perpetual tribute to his power. Mr. Waddington had nothing like the same complacence in thinking of his own son Horace; but then Horace's existence and his activity were not a tribute but a menace, a standing danger, not only to his power but to his fascination, his sense of himself as a still young, still brilliant and effective personality. (Horace inherited his mother's deplorable lack of seriousness.) And it was in Mrs. Levitt's society that Mr. Waddington was most conscious of his youth, his brilliance and effect. With an agreeable sense of anticipation he climbed up the slopes of Sheep Street and Park Street, and so into the Square.

The house, muffled in ivy, hid discreetly in the far corner, behind the two tall elms on the Green. Mrs. Trinder, the landlady, had a sidelong bend of the head and a smile that acknowledged him as Mr. Waddington of Wyck and Mrs. Levitt's benefactor.

And as he waited in the low, mullion-darkened room he reminded himself that he had come to refuse her request. If, as he suspected, it was the Ballingers' cottage that she wanted. To be sure, the Ballingers had notice to quit in June, but he couldn't very well turn the Ballingers out if they wanted to stay, when there wasn't a decent house in the place to turn them into. He would have to make this very clear to Mrs. Levitt.

Not that he approved of Ballinger. The fellow, one of his best farm hands, had behaved infamously, first of all demanding preposterous wages, and then, just because Mr. Waddington had refused to be brow-beaten, leaving his service for Colonel Grainger's. Colonel Grainger had behaved infamously, buying Foss Bank with the money he had made in high explosives, and then letting fly his confounded Socialism all over the county. Knowing nothing, mind you, about local conditions, and actually raising the rate of wages without consulting anybody, and upsetting the farm labourers for miles round. At a time when the prosperity of the entire country depended on the farmers. Still, Mr. Waddington was not the man to take a petty revenge on his inferiors. He didn't blame Ballinger; he blamed Colonel Grainger. He would like to see Grainger boycotted by the whole county.

The door opened. He strode forward and found himself holding out a sudden, fervid hand to a lady who was not Mrs. Levitt. He drew up, turning his gesture into a bow, rather unnecessarily ceremonious; but he could not annihilate instantaneously all that fervour.

"I am Mrs. Levitt's sister, Mrs. Rickards. Mr. Waddington, is it not? I'll tell Elise you're here. I know she'll be glad to see you. She has been very much upset."

She remained standing before him long enough for him to be aware of a projecting bust, of white serge, of smartness, of purplish copper hair, a raking panama's white brim, of eyebrows, a rouged smile, and a smell of orris root. Before he could grasp its connexion with Mrs. Levitt this amazing figure had disappeared and given place to a tapping of heels and a furtive, scuffling laugh on the stairs outside. A shriller laugh—that must be Mrs. Rickards—a long Sh-sh-sh! Then the bang of the front door covering the lady's retreat, and Mrs. Levitt came in, stifling merriment under a minute pocket-handkerchief.

He took it in then. They were sisters, Mrs. Rickards and Elise Levitt. Elise, if you cared to be critical, had the same defects: short legs, loose hips; the same exaggerations: the toppling breasts underpinned by the shafts of her stays. Not Mr. Waddington's taste. And yet—and yet Elise had contrived a charming and handsome effect out of black eyes and the milk-white teeth in the ivory-white face. The play of the black eyebrows distracted you from the equine bend of the nose that sprang between them; the movements of her mouth, the white flash of its smile, made you forget its thinness and hardness and the slight heaviness of its jaw. Something foreign about her. Something French. Piquant. And then, her clothes. Mrs. Levitt wore a coat and skirt, her sister's white serge with a distinction, a greyish stripe or something; clean straightness that stiffened and fined down her exuberance. One jewel, one bit of gold, and she might have been vulgar. But no. He thought: she knows what becomes her. Immaculate purity of white gloves, white shoes, white panama; and the black points of the ribbon, of her eyebrows, her eyes and hair. After all, the sort of woman Mr. Waddington liked to be seen out walking with. She made him feel slender.

"My *dear* Mr. Waddington, how good of you!"

"My dear Mrs. Levitt—always delighted—when it's possible—to do anything."

As she covered him with her brilliant eyes he tightened his shoulders and stood firm, while his spirit braced itself against persuasion. If it was the Ballingers' cottage—

"I really am ashamed of myself. I never seem to send for you unless I'm in trouble."

"Isn't that the time?" His voice thickened. "So long as you do send—" He thought: It isn't the Ballingers' cottage then.

"It's your own fault. You've always been so good, so kind. To my poor Toby."

"Nothing to do with Toby, I hope, the trouble?"

"Oh, no. No. And yet in a way it has. I'm afraid, Mr. Waddington, I may have to leave."

"To leave? Leave Wyck?"

"Leave dear Wyck."

"Not seriously?"

He wasn't prepared for that. The idea hit him hard in a place that he hadn't thought was tender.

"Quite seriously."

"Dear me. This is very distressing. Very distressing indeed. But you would not take such a step without consulting your friends?"

"I *am* consulting you."

"Yes, yes. But have you thought it well over?"

"Thinking isn't any use. I shall have to, unless something can be done."

He thought: "Financial difficulties. Debts. An expensive lady. Unless something could be done?" He didn't know that he was exactly prepared to do it. But his tongue answered in spite of him.

"Something must be done. We can't let you go like this, my dear lady."

"That's it. I don't see how I *can* go, with dear Toby here. Nor yet how I'm to stay."

"Won't you tell me what the trouble is?"

"The trouble is that Mrs. Trinder's son's just been demobilized, and she wants our rooms for his wife and family."

"Come—surely we can find other rooms."

"All the best ones are taken. There's nothing left that I'd care to live in…. Besides, it isn't rooms I want, Mr. Waddington, it's a house."

It was, of course, the Ballingers' cottage. But she couldn't have it. She couldn't have it.

"I wouldn't mind how small it was. If only I had a little home of my own. You don't know, Mr. Waddington, what it is to be without a home of your own. I haven't had a home for years. Five years. Not since the war."

"I'm afraid," said Mr. Waddington, "at present there isn't a house for you in Wyck."

He brooded earnestly, as though he were trying to conjure up, to create out of nothing, a house for her and a home.

"No. But I understand that the Ballingers will be leaving in June. You said that at any time, if you had a house, I should have it."

"I said a house, Mrs. Levitt, not a cottage."

"It's all the same to me. The Ballingers' cottage could be made into an adorable little house."

"It could. With a few hundred pounds spent on it."

"Well, you'd be improving your property, wouldn't you? And you'd get it back in the higher rent."

"I'm not thinking about getting anything back. And nothing would please me better. Only, you see, I can't very well turn Ballinger out as long as he behaves himself."

"I wouldn't have him turned out for the world…. But do you consider that Ballinger *has* behaved himself?"

"Well, he played me a dirty trick, perhaps, when he went to Grainger; but if Grainger can afford to pay for him I've no right to object to his being bought. It isn't a reason for turning the man out."

"I don't see how he can expect you to refuse a good tenant for him."

"I must if I haven't a good house to put him into."

"He doesn't expect it, Mr. Waddington. Didn't you give him notice in December?"

"A mere matter of form. He knows he can stay on if there's nowhere else for him to go to."

"Then why," said Mrs. Levitt, "does he go about saying that he dares you to let the cottage over his head?"

"Does he? Does he say that?"

"He says he'll pay you out. He'll summons you. He was most abusive."

Mr. Waddington's face positively swelled with the choleric flush that swamped its genial fatuity.

"It seems somebody told him you were going to do up the cottage and let it for more rent."

"I don't know who could have spread that story."

"I assure you, Mr. Waddington, it wasn't me!"

"My dear Mrs. Levitt, of course…. I won't say I wasn't thinking of it, and that I wouldn't have done it, if I could have got rid of Ballinger…." He meditated.

"I don't see why I shouldn't get rid of him. If he dares me, the scoundrel, he's simply asking for it. And he shall have it."

"Oh, but I wouldn't for worlds have him turned into the street. With his wife and babies."

"My dear lady, I shan't turn them into the street. I shouldn't be allowed to. There's a cottage at Lower Wyck they can go into. The one he had when he first came to me."

He wondered why he hadn't thought of it before. It wasn't, as it stood, a decent cottage; but if he was prepared to spend fifty pounds or so on it, it could be made habitable; and, by George, he *was* prepared, if it was only to teach Ballinger a lesson. For it meant that Ballinger would have to walk an extra mile up hill to his work every day. Serve him right, the impudent rascal.

"Poor thing, he won't," said Mrs. Levitt, "have his nice garden."

"He won't. Ballinger must learn," said Mr. Waddington with magisterial severity, "that he can't have everything. He certainly can't have it both ways.

Abuse and threaten me and expect favours. He may go ... to Colonel Grainger."

"If it really *must* happen," said Mrs. Levitt, "do you mean that I may have the house?"

"I shall be only too delighted to have such a charming tenant."

"Well, I shan't threaten and abuse you and call you every nasty name under the sun. And you won't, you *won't* turn me out when my lease is up?"

He bowed over the hand she held out to him.

"You shall never be turned out as long as you want to stay."

By twelve o'clock they had arranged the details; Mr. Waddington was to put in a bathroom; to throw the two rooms on the ground floor into one; to build out a new sitting-room with a bedroom over it; and to paint and distemper the place, in cream white, throughout. And it was to be called the White House. By the time they had finished with it Ballinger's cottage had become the house Mrs. Levitt had dreamed of all her life, and not unlike the house Mr. Waddington had dreamed of that minute (while he planned the bathroom); the little bijou house where an adorable but not too rigorously moral lady—He stopped with a mental jerk, ashamed. He had no reason to suppose that Elise was or would become such a lady.

And the poor innocent woman was saying, "Just one thing, Mr. Waddington, the rent?"

(No earthly reason.) "We can talk about that another time. I shan't be hard on you."

No. He wouldn't be hard on her. But in that other case there wouldn't have been any rent at all.

As he left the house he could see Mrs. Rickards hurrying towards it across the square.

"She waddles like a duck," he thought. The movement suggested a plebeian excitement and curiosity that displeased him. He recalled her face. Her extraordinary face. "Quite enough," he thought, "to put all that into my head. Poor Elise"

He liked to think of her. It made him feel what he had felt last night over Barbara Madden—virtuous—as though he had struggled and got the better of an impetuous passion. He was so touched by his own beautiful renunciation that when he found Fanny working in the garden he felt a sudden tenderness for her as the cause of it. She looked up at him from her pansy bed and laughed. "What are you looking so sentimental for, old thing?"

3

Mrs. Levitt's affair settled, he could now give his whole time to the serious business of the day.

He was exceedingly anxious to get it over. Nothing could be more disturbing than Fanny's suggestion that the name of Sir John Corbett might carry more weight with his Committee than his own. The Waddingtons of Wyck had ancestry. Waddingtons had held Lower Wyck Manor for ten generations, whereas Sir John Corbett's father had bought Underwoods and rebuilt it somewhere in the 'seventies. On the other hand Sir John was the largest and richest landowner in the place. He could buy up Wyck—on—the—Hill to—morrow and thrive on the transaction. He therefore represented the larger vested interest And as the whole object of the League was the safeguarding of vested interests, in other words, of liberty, that British liberty which is bound up with law and order, with private property in general and landownership in particular; as the principle of its very being was the preservation of precisely such an institution as Sir John himself, the Committee of the Wyck Branch of the League could hardly avoid inviting him to be its president. There was no blinking the fact, and Fanny hadn't blinked it, that Sir John was the proper person. Most of Fanny's suggestions had a strong but unpleasant element of common sense.

But the more interest he took in the League, the more passionately he flung himself into the business of its creation, the more abhorrent to Mr. Waddington was the thought that the chief place in it, the presidency, would pass over his head to Sir John.

His only hope was in Sir John's well-known indolence and irresponsibility. Sir John was the exhausted reaction from the efforts of a self-made grandfather and of a father spendthrift in energy; he had had everything done for him ever since he was a baby, and consequently was now unable or unwilling to do anything for himself or other people. You couldn't see him taking an active part in the management of the League, and Mr. Waddington couldn't see himself doing all the work and handing over all the glory to Sir John. Still, between Mr. Waddington and the glory there was only this supine figure of Sir John, and Sir John once out of the running he could count without immodesty on the unanimous vote of any committee he formed in Wyck.

It was possible that even a Sir John Corbett would not really carry it over a Waddington of Wyck, but Mr. Waddington wasn't taking any risks. What he had to do was to suggest the presidency to Sir John in such a way that he would be certain to refuse it.

He had the good luck to find Sir John alone in his library at tea-time, eating hot buttered toast.

There was hope for Mr. Waddington in Sir John's attitude, lying back and nursing his little round stomach, hope in the hot, buttery gleam of his cheeks, in his wide mouth, lazy under the jutting grey moustache, and in the scrabbling of his little legs as he exerted himself to stand upright.

"Well, Waddington, glad to see you."

He was in his chair again. With another prodigious effort he leaned forward and rang for more tea and more toast.

"Did you walk?" said Sir John. His little round eyes expressed horror at the possibility.

"No, I just ran over in my car."

"Drove yourself?"

"No. Too much effort of attention. I find it interferes with my thinking."

"Interferes with everything," said Sir John. "'Spect you drove enough during the war to last you for the rest of your life."

"Ah, Government service. A very different thing. That reminds me; I've come to-day to consult you on a matter of public business."

"Business?" (He noted Sir John's uneasy pout.) "Better have some tea first." Sir John took another piece of buttered toast.

If only Sir John would go on eating. Nothing like buttered toast for sustaining that mood of voluptuous inertia.

When Mr. Waddington judged the moment propitious he began. "While I was up in London I had the pleasure of lunching with Sir Maurice Gedge. He wants me to start a branch of the National League of Liberty here."

"Liberty? Shouldn't have thought that was much in your line. Didn't expect to see you waving the red flag, what? Why didn't you put him on to our friend Grainger?"

"My dear Corbett, what are you thinking of? The object of the League is to put down all that sort of thing—Socialism—Bolshevism—to rouse the whole country and get it to stand solid for order and good government."

"H'm. Is it? Queer sort of title for a thing of that sort—League of Liberty, what?"

Mr. Waddington raised a clenched fist. Already in spirit he was on his platform. "Exactly the title that's needed. The people want liberty, always have wanted it. We'll let 'em have it. True liberty. British liberty. I tell you, Corbett, we're out against the tyranny of Labour minorities. You and I and every man that's got any standing and any influence, we've got to see to it that we don't have a revolution and Communism and a Soviet Government here."

"Come, you don't think the Bolshies are as strong as all that, do you?"

Mr. Waddington brought his fist down on the arm of his chair. "I *know* they are," he said. "And look here—if they get the upper hand, it's the great capitalists, the great property holders, the great _land_owners like you and me, Corbett, who'll be the first to suffer…. Why, we're suffering as it is, here in Wyck, with just the little that fellow Grainger can do. The time'll come, mark my words, when we shan't be able to get a single labourer to work for us for a fair wage. They'll bleed us white, Corbett, before they've done with us, if we don't make a stand, and make it now.

"That's what the League's for, to set up a standard, something we can point to and say: These are the principles we stand for. Something you can rally the whole country round. We shall want your support—"

"I shall be very glad—anything I can do—"

Mr. Waddington was a little disturbed by this ready acquiescence.

"Mind you, it isn't going to end here, in Wyck. I shall start it in Wyck first; then I shall take it straight to the big towns, Gloucester, Cheltenham, Cirencester, Nailsworth, Stroud. We'll set 'em going till we've got a branch in every town and every village in the county."

He thought: "That ought to settle him." He had created a vision of intolerable activity.

"Bless me," said Sir John, "you've got your work cut out for you."

"Of course I shall have to get a local committee first. I can't take a step like that without consulting you."

Sir John muttered something that sounded like "Very good of you, I'm sure."

"No more than my duty to the League. Now, the point is, Sir Maurice was anxious that *I* should be president of this local branch. It needs somebody with energy and determination—the president's work, certainly, will be cut out for him—and I feel very strongly, and I think that my Committee will feel that *you*, Corbett, are the proper person."

"H'm—m."

"I didn't think I should be justified in going further without first obtaining your consent."

"We-ell—"

Mr. Waddington's anxiety was almost unbearable. The programme had evidently appealed to Sir John. Supposing, after all, he accepted?

"I wouldn't ask you to undertake anything so—so arduous, but that it'll strengthen my hands with my Committee; in fact, I may get a much stronger and more influential Committee if I can come to them, and tell them beforehand that you have consented to be president."

"I don't mind being president," said Sir John, "if I haven't got to do anything."

"I'm afraid—I'm *afraid* we couldn't allow you to be a mere figurehead."

"But presidents always are figureheads, aren't they?"

There was a bantering gleam in Sir John's eyes that irritated Mr. Waddington. That was the worst of Corbett; you couldn't get him to take a serious thing seriously.

"'T any rate," Sir John went on, "there's always some secretary johnnie who runs round and does the work."

So that was Corbett's idea: to sit in his armchair and bag all the prestige, while he, Waddington of Wyck, ran round and did the work.

"Not in this case. In these small local affairs you can't delegate business. Everything depends on the personal activity of the president."

"The deuce it does. How do you mean?"

"I mean this. If Sir John Corbett asks for a subscription he gets it. We've got to round up the whole county and all the townspeople and villagers. It's no use shooting pamphlets at 'em from a motor-car. They like being personally interviewed. If Sir John Corbett comes and talk to them and tells them they must join, ten to one they will join.

"And there isn't any time to be lost if we want to get in first before other places take it up. It'll mean pretty sharp work, day in and day out, rounding them all up."

"Oh, Lord, Waddington, *don't*. I'm tired already with the bare idea of it."

"Come, we can't have you tired, Corbett. Why, it won't be worse, it won't be half as bad as a season's hunting. You're just the man for it. Fit as fit."

"Not half as fit as I look, Waddington."

"There's another thing—the meetings. If the posters say Sir John Corbett will address the meeting people'll come. If Sir John Corbett speaks they'll listen."

"My dear fellow, that settles it. I can't speak for nuts. You *know* I can't. I can introduce a speaker and move a vote of thanks, and that's about all I *can* do. It's your show, not mine. *You* ought to be president, Waddington. You'll enjoy it and I shan't."

"I don't know at all about enjoying it. It'll be infernally hard work."

"Precisely."

"You don't mean, Corbett, that you won't come in with us? That you won't come on the Committee?"

"I'll come on all right if I haven't got to speak, and if I haven't got to do anything. I shan't be much good, but I could at least propose you as president. You couldn't very well propose yourself."

"It's very good of you."

Mr. Waddington made his voice sound casual and indifferent, so that he might appear to be entertaining the suggestion provisionally and under protest. "There'll have to be one big meeting before the Committee's formed or anything. If I let you off the presidency," he said playfully, "will you take the chair?"

"For that one evening?"

"That one evening only."

"You'll do all the talking?"

"I shall have to."

"All right, my dear fellow. I daresay I can get my wife to come on your committee, too. That'll help you to rope in the townspeople.... And now, supposing we drop it and have a quiet smoke."

He roused himself to one more effort. "Of course, we'll send you a subscription, both of us."

Mr. Waddington drove off from Underwoods in a state of pleasurable elation. He had got what he wanted without appearing—without appearing at all to be playing for it. Corbett had never spotted him.

There he was wrong. At that very moment Sir John was relating the incident to Lady Corbett.

"And you could see all the time the fellow wanted it himself. I put him in an awful funk, pretending I was going to take it."

All the same, he admitted very handsomely that the idea of the League was "topping," and that Waddington was the man for it. And the subscription that he and Lady Corbett sent was very handsome, too. Unfortunately it obliged Mr. Waddington to contribute a slightly larger sum, by way of maintaining his ascendancy.

4

On his way home he called at the Old Dower House in the Square to see his mother. He had arranged to meet Fanny and Barbara Madden there and drive them home.

The old lady was sitting in her chair, handsome, with dark eyes still brilliant in her white Roman face, a small imperious face, yet soft, soft in its network of fine grooves and pittings. An exquisite old lady in a black satin gown and white embroidered shawl, with a white Chantilly scarf binding rolled masses of white hair. She had been a Miss Postlethwaite, of Medlicott.

"My dear boy—so you've got back?"

She turned to her son with a soft moan of joy, lifting up her hands to hold his face as he stooped to kiss her.

"How well you look," she said. "Is that London or coming back to Fanny?"

"It's coming back to you."

"Ah, she hasn't spoilt you. You know how to say nice things to your old mother."

She looked up at him, at his solemn face that simmered with excited egoism. Barbara could see that he was playing—playing in his ponderous, fatuous way, at being her young, her not more than twenty-five years old son. He turned with a sudden, sportive, caracoling movement, to find a chair for himself. He was sitting on it now, close beside his mother, and she was holding one of his big, fleshy hands in her fragile bird claws and patting it.

From her study of the ancestral portraits in the Manor dining-room Barbara gathered that he owed to his mother the handsome Roman structure that held up his face, after all, so proudly through its layers of Waddington flesh. He had the Postlethwaite nose. The old lady looked at her, gratified by the grave attention of her eyes.

"Miss Madden can't believe that a little woman like me could have such a great big son," she said. "But, you see, he isn't big to me. He'll never be any older than thirteen."

You could see it. If he wasn't really thirteen to her he wasn't a day older than twenty-five; he was her young grown-up son whose caresses flattered her.

"She spoils me, Miss Madden."

You could see that it pleased him to sit close to her knees, to have his hand patted and be spoilt.

"Nonsense. Now tell me what happened at Underwoods. Is it to be John Corbett or you?"

"Corbett says it's to be me."

"I'm glad he's had that much sense. Well—and now tell me all about this League of yours."

He told her all about it, and she sat very quietly, listening, nodding her proud old head in approval. He talked about it till it was time to go. Then the old lady became agitated.

"My dear boy, you mustn't let Kimber drive you too fast down that hill. Fanny, will you tell Kimber to be careful?"

Her face trembled with anxiety as she held it to him to be kissed. At that moment he was her child, escaping from her, going out rashly into the dangerous world.

"I like going to see Granny," said Fanny as Kimber tucked them up together in the car. "She makes me feel young."

"You may very well feel it," said Mr. Waddington. "It's only my mother's white hair, Miss Madden, that makes her look old."

"I thought," said Barbara, "she looked ever so much younger"—she was going to say, "than she is"—"than most people's mothers."

"You will have noticed," Fanny said, "that my husband is younger than most people."

Barbara noticed that he had drawn himself up with an offended air, unnaturally straight. He didn't like it, this discussion about ages.

They were running out of the Square when Fanny remembered and cried out, "Oh, stop him, Horatio. We must go back and see if Ralph's coming to dinner."

But at the White Hart they were told that Mr. Bevan had "gone to Oxford on his motor-bike" and was not expected to return before ten o'clock.

"Sorry, Barbara."

"I don't see why you should apologize to Miss Madden, my dear. I've no doubt she can get on very well without him."

"She may want something rather more exciting than you and me, sometimes."

"I'm quite happy," Barbara said.

"Of course you're happy. It isn't everybody who enjoys Ralph Bevan's society. I daresay you're like me; you find him a great hindrance to serious conversation."

"That's why *I* enjoy him," Fanny said. "We'll ask him for to-morrow night."

Barbara tucked her chin into the collar of her coat. The car was running down Sheep Street into Lower Wyck. She stared out abstractedly at the eastern valley, the delicate green cornfields and pink fallows, the muffling of dim trees, all washed in the pale eastern blue, rolling out and up to the blue ridge.

It made her happy to look at it. It made her happy to think of Ralph Bevan coming to-morrow. If it had been to-night it would have been all over in three hours. And something—she was not sure what, but felt that it might be Mr. Waddington—something would have cut in to spoil the happiness of it. But now she had it to think about, and her thoughts were safe. "What are you thinking about, Barbara?"

"The view," said Barbara. "I want to sketch it."

V

1

Mr. Waddington was in his library, drawing up his prospectus while Fanny and Barbara Madden looked on. At Fanny's suggestion (he owned magnanimously that it was a good one) he had decided to "sail in," as she called it, with the prospectus first, not only before he formed his Committee, but before he held his big meeting. (They had fixed the date of it for that day month, Saturday, June the twenty-first.)

"You come before them from the beginning," she said, "with something fixed and definite that they can't go back on." And by signing the prospectus, Horatio Bysshe Waddington, he identified it beyond all contention with himself.

It was at this point that Barbara had blundered.

"Why," she had said, "should we go to all that bother and expense? Why can't we send out the original prospectus?"

"My dear Barbara, the original prospectus isn't any good."

"Why isn't it?"

"Because it isn't Horatio's prospectus."

Barbara looked down and away from the dangerous light in Fanny's eyes.

"But it expresses his views, doesn't it?"

"That's no good when he wants to express them himself."

And so far from being any good, the original prospectus was a positive hindrance to Mr. Waddington. It took all the wind out of his sails; it took, as he justly complained, the very words out of his mouth and the ideas out of his head; it got in his way and upset him at every turn. Somehow or other he had got to stamp his personality upon this thing. "It's no good," he said; "if they can't recognize it as a personal appeal from ME." And here it was, stamped all over, and indelibly, with the personalities of Sir Maurice Gedge and his London Committee. And he couldn't depart radically from the lines they had laid down; there were just so many things to be said, and Sir Maurice and his Committee had contrived to say them all.

But, though the matter was given him, Mr. Waddington, before he actually tackled his prospectus, had conceived himself as supplying his own fresh and inimitable manner; the happy touch, the sudden, arresting turn. But somehow it wasn't working out that way. Try as he would, he couldn't get away from the turns and touches supplied by Sir Maurice Gedge.

"It would have been easy enough," he said, "to draw up the original prospectus. I'd a thousand times rather do that than write one on the top of it."

Fanny agreed. "It's got to *look* different," she said, "without *being* different."

"Couldn't we," said Barbara, "turn it upside down?"

"Upside down?" He stared at her with great owl's eyes, offended, suspecting her this time of an outrageous levity.

"Yes. Really upside down. You see, the heads go in this order—Defence of Private Property; Defence of Capital; Defence of Liberty; Defence of Government; Defence of the Empire; Danger of Revolution, Communism and Bolshevism; Every Man's Duty. Why not reverse them? Every Man's Duty; Danger of Bolshevism, Communism and Revolution; Defence of the Empire; Defence of Government; Defence of Liberty; Defence of Capital; Defence of Private Property."

"That's an idea," said Fanny.

"Not at all a bad idea," said Mr. Waddington. "You might take down the heads in that order."

Barbara took them down, and it was agreed that they presented a very original appearance thus reversed; and, as Barbara pointed out, the one order was every bit as logical as the other; and though Mr. Waddington objected that he would have preferred to close on the note of Government and Empire, he was open to the suggestion that, while this might appeal more to the county, with the farmers and townspeople, capital and private property would strike further home. And by the time he had changed "combat the forces of disorder" to "take a stand against anarchy and disruption," and "spirit of freedom in this country" to "British genius for liberty," and "darkest hour in England's history" to "blackest period in the history of England," he was persuaded that the prospectus was now entirely and absolutely his own.

"But I think we must sound the note of hope to end up with. My own message. How about 'We must remember that the darkest hour comes before dawn'?"

"My dear Horatio, if you inflate yourself so over your prospectus, you'll have no wind left when you come to speak. Be as wildly original as you please, but *don't* be wasteful and extravagant."

"All right, Fanny. I will reserve the dawn. Please make a note of that, Miss Madden. Speech. 'Blackest'—or did I say 'darkest'?—'hour before dawn.'"

"You'd better reserve all you can," said Fanny.

When Barbara had typed the prospectus, Mr. Waddington insisted on taking it to Pyecraft himself. He wanted to insure its being printed without delay, and to arrange for the posters and handbills; he also wanted to see the impression it would make on Pyecraft and on the young lady in Pyecraft's shop. He liked to think of the stir in the composing room when it was handed in, and of the importance he was conferring on Pyecraft.

"You haven't said what you think of the prospectus," said Fanny, as they watched him go.

"I haven't said what I think of the League of Liberty."

"What *do* you think of it?"

"I think it looks as if somebody was in an awful funk; and I don't see that there's going to be much liberty about it."

"That," said Fanny, "is how it struck me. But it'll keep Horatio quiet for the next six months."

"*Quiet?* And afterwards?"

"Oh, afterwards there'll be his book."

"I'd forgotten his book."

"That'll keep him quieter than anything else; if you can get him to settle down to it."

2

That evening Barbara witnessed the reconciliation of Mr. Waddington and Ralph Bevan. Mr. Waddington made a spectacle of it, standing, majestic and immovable, by his hearth and holding out his hand long before Ralph had got near enough to take it.

"Good evening, Ralph. Glad to see you here again."

"Good of you to ask me, sir."

Barbara thought he winced a little at the "sir." He had a distaste for those forms of deference which implied his seniority. You could see he didn't like Ralph. His voice was genial, but there was no light in his bulging stare; the heavy lines of his face never lifted. She wondered: Was it Ralph's brilliant youth that had offended him, reminding him, even when he refused to recognize his fascination? For you could see that he did refuse, that he regarded Ralph Bevan as an inferior, insignificant personality. Barbara had to revise her theory. He wasn't jealous of him. It would never occur to him that Fanny, or Barbara for that matter, could find Ralph interesting. Nothing could disturb for a moment his immense satisfaction with himself. He conducted dinner with a superb detachment, confining his attention to Fanny and Barbara, as if he were pretending that Ralph wasn't there, until suddenly he heard Fanny asking him if he knew anything about the National League of Liberty and what he thought of it.

"Mr. Waddington doesn't want to know what I think of it."

"No, but we want to."

"My dear Fanny, any opinion, any honest opinion—"

"Oh, Ralph's opinion will be honest enough."

"Honest, I daresay," said Mr. Waddington.

"Well, if you really want to know, I think it's a pathological symptom."

"A what?" said Mr. Waddington, startled into a show of interest.

"Pathological symptom. It's all funk. Blue funk. True blue funk."

"That's what Barbara says."

The young man looked at Barbara as much as to say, "I knew I could trust you to take the only intelligent view."

"It's run," he said, "by a few imbeciles, like Sir Maurice Gedge. They're scared out of their lives of Bolshevism."

"Do you mean to say that Bolshevism isn't dangerous?"

"Not in this country."

"Perhaps, then, you'd like to see a Soviet Government in this country?"

"I didn't say so."

"But I understand that you uphold Bolshevism?"

"I don't uphold funk. But," said Ralph, "there's rather more in it than that. It's being engineered. It's a deliberate, dishonest, and malicious attempt to discredit Labour."

"Absurd," said Mr. Waddington. "You show that you are ignorant of the very principles of the League."

If he recognized Ralph's youth, it was only to despise it as crude and uninformed.

"It is—the—National—League—of Liberty."

"Well, that's about all the liberty there is in it—liberty to suppress liberty."

"You may not know that I'm starting a branch of the League in Wyck."

"I'm sorry, sir. I did not know. Fanny, why did you lay that trap for me?"

"Because I wanted your real opinion."

"Before you set up an opinion, you had better come to my meeting on the twenty-first. Then perhaps you'll learn something about it."

Fanny changed the subject to Sir John Corbett's laziness.

"A man," said Mr. Waddington, "without any seriousness, any sense of responsibility."

After coffee Mr. Waddington removed Fanny to the library to consult with him about the formation of his Committee, leaving Barbara and Ralph Bevan alone. Fanny waved her hand to them from the doorway, signalling her blessing on their unrestrained communion.

"It's deplorable," said Ralph, "to see a woman of Fanny's intelligence mixing herself up with a rotten scheme like that."

"Poor darling, she only does it to keep him quiet."

"Oh, yes, I admit there's every excuse for her."

They looked at each other and smiled. A smile of delicious and secret understanding.

"Isn't he wonderful?" she said.

"I thought you'd like him.... I say, you know, I *must* come to his meeting. He'll be more wonderful than ever there. Can't you see him?"

"I can. It's almost *too* much—to think that I should be allowed to know him, to live in the same house with him, to have him turning himself on by the hour together. What have I done to deserve it?"

"I see," he said, "you *have* got it."

"Got what?"

"The taste for him. The genuine passion. I had it when I was here. I couldn't have stood it if I hadn't."

"I know. You must have had it. You've got it now."

"And I don't suppose I've seen him anything like at his best. You'll get more out of him than I did."

"Oh, do you think I shall?"

"Yes. He may rise to greater heights."

"You mean he may go to greater lengths?"

"Perhaps. I don't know. You'd have, of course, to stop his lengths, which would be a pity. I think of him mostly in heights. There's no reason why you shouldn't let him soar.... But I mustn't discuss him. I've just eaten his dinner."

"No, we mustn't," Barbara agreed. "That's the worst of dinners."

"I say, though, can't we meet somewhere?"

"Where we *can?*"

"Yes. Where we can let ourselves rip? Couldn't we go for more walks together?"

"I'm afraid there won't be time."

"There'll be loads of time. When he's off in his car 'rounding up the county.'"

"When he's 'off,' I'm 'on' as Mrs. Waddington's companion."

"Fanny won't mind. She'll let you do anything you like. At any rate, she'll let *me* do anything *I* like."

"Will you ask her?"

"Of course I shall."

So they settled it.

3

When Barbara said to herself that Mr. Waddington would spoil her evening with Ralph Bevan, she had judged by the change that had come over the house since the return of its master. You felt it first in the depressed faces of the servants, of Partridge and Annie Trinder. A thoughtful gloom had settled even on Kimber. Worse than all, Fanny Waddington had left off humming. Barbara missed that spontaneous expression of her happiness.

She thought: "What is it he does to them?" And yet it was clear that he didn't do anything. They were simply crushed by the sheer mass and weight of his egoism. He imposed on them somehow his incredible consciousness of himself. He left an atmosphere of uneasiness. You felt it when he wasn't there; even when Fanny had settled down in the drawing-room with "Tono-Bungay" you felt her fear that at any minute the door would open and Horatio would come in.

But Barbara wasn't depressed. She enjoyed the perpetual spectacle he made. She enjoyed his very indifference to Ralph, his refusal to see that he could command attention, his conviction of his own superior fascination. She knew now what Ralph meant when he said it would be unkind to spoil him for her. He was to burst on her without preparation or description. She was to discover him first of all herself. First of all. But she could see the time coming when her chief joy would be their making him out, bit by bit, together. She even discerned a merry devil in Fanny that amused itself at Horatio's expense; that was aware of Barbara's amusement and condoned it. There were ultimate decencies that prevented any open communion with Fanny. But beyond that refusal to smile at Horatio after eating his dinner, she could see no decencies restraining Ralph. She could count on him when her private delight became intolerable and must be shared.

But there were obstacles to their intercourse. Mr. Waddington couldn't very well start on what he called his "campaign" until he was armed with his prospectus, and Pyecraft took more than a week to print it. And while she sat idle, thinking of her salary, the fiend of conscience prompted Barbara to ask him for work. Wasn't there his book?

"My book? My Cotswold book?" He pretended he had forgotten all about it. He waved it away. "The book is only a recreation, an amusement. Plenty of time for that when I've got my League going. Still, I shall be glad when I can settle down to it, again.".... He was considering it now with reminiscent affection.... "If it would amuse you to look at it—"

He began a fussy search in his bureau.

"Ah, here we are!"

He unearthed two piles of manuscript, one typed, the other written, both scored with erasures, with almost illegible corrections and insertions.

"It's in a terrible mess," he said.

She saw what her work would be: to cut a way through the jungle, to make clearings.

"If I were to type it all over again, you'd have a clean copy to work on when you were ready."

"If you *would* be so good. It's that young rascal Ralph. He'd no business to leave it in that state."

Her scruple came again to Barbara.

"Mr. Waddington, you'd take him on again for your secretary if he'd come back?"

"He'd come back all right. Trust him."

"And you'd take him?"

"My dear young lady, why should I? I don't want *him*; I want *you*."

"And *I* don't want to stand in his way."

"You needn't worry about that."

"I can't help worrying about it. You'd take him back if I wasn't here."

"You *are* here."

"But if I weren't?"

"Come, come. You mustn't talk to me like that."

She went away and talked to Fanny.

"I can't bear doing him out of his job. If he'll come back—"

"My dear, you don't know Ralph. He'd die rather than come back. They've made it impossible between them."

"Mr. Waddington says he'd take him back if I wasn't here."

"He wouldn't. He only thinks he would, because it makes him feel magnanimous. He offered Ralph half a year's salary if he'd go at once. And Ralph went at once and wouldn't touch the salary. That made him come out top dog, and Horatio didn't like it. Not that he supposed he could score off Ralph with money. He isn't vulgar."

No. He wasn't vulgar. But she wondered how he would camouflage it to himself—that insult to his pride. And there was Ralph's pride that was so fiery and so clean. Yet—

"Yet Mr. Bevan comes and dines," she said.

"Yes, he comes and dines. He'll always be my cousin, though he won't be Horatio's secretary. He's got a very sweet nature and he keeps the issues clear."

"But what will he *do*? He can't live on his sweet nature."

"Oh, he's got enough to live on, though not enough to—to do what he wants on. But he'll get a job all right. You needn't bother your dear little head about Ralph."

Fanny said to herself: "I'll tell him, then he'll adore her more than ever. If only he adores her *enough* he'll buck up and get something to do."

VI

1

Mr. Waddington did not approve of Mrs. Levitt's intimacy with her sister, Bertha Rickards.

He would have approved of it still less if he had heard the conversation which Mrs. Trinder heard and reported to Miss Gregg, the governess at the rectory, who told the Rector's wife, who told the Rector, who told Colonel Grainger, who told Ralph Sevan, who kept it to himself.

"What did you say to the old boy, Elise?"

"Don't ask me what I *said!*"

"Well—have you got the cottage?"

"Of course I've got it, silly cuckoo. I can get anything out of him I like. He wasn't going to turn those Ballingers out, but I made him."

"Did he say when Mrs. Waddington was going to call?"

Bertha couldn't resist the temptation of pinching where she knew the flesh was tender.

"I didn't ask him."

"She can't very well be off it, now he's your landlord."

That was what Mrs. Levitt thought. And if Mrs. Waddington called, Lady Corbett couldn't very well be off it either. They were the only ones in Wyck who had not called; but it would be futile to pretend that they didn't matter, that they were not the ones who mattered more than anybody.

The net she had drawn round Mr. Waddington was tightening, though he was as yet unaware of his entanglement. First of all, the Lower Wyck cottage was put into thorough repair; and if the plaster was not quite dry when the Ballingers moved into it, that was not Mr. Waddington's concern. He had provided them with a house, which was all that the law could reasonably require him to do. Clearly it was Hitchin, the builder, who should be held responsible for the plaster, not he. As for the rheumatism Mrs. Ballinger got, supposing it could be put down to the damp plaster and not to some inherent defect in Mrs. Ballinger's constitution, clearly that was not Mr. Waddington's concern either. If anybody was responsible for Mrs. Ballinger's rheumatism, it was Hitchin.

Mr. Waddington did not approve of Hitchin. Hitchin was a Socialist who followed Colonel Grainger's lead in overpaying his workmen, with disastrous consequences to other people; for over and above the general upsetting caused by this gratuitous interference with the prevailing economic system, Mr. Hitchin was in the habit of recouping himself by monstrous overcharges. And Mr. Hitchin was not only the best builder in the neighbourhood, but the only builder and stonemason in Wyck-on-the-Hill, so that he had you practically at his mercy.

And operations at the Sheep Street cottage were suspended while Mr. Waddington disputed Mr. Hitchin's estimate bit by bit, from the total cost of building the new rooms down to the last pot of enamel paint and his charge per foot for lead piping. June was slipping away while they contended, and there seemed little chance of Mrs. Levitt's getting into her house before Michaelmas, if then.

So that on the morning of the nineteenth, two days before the meeting, Mr. Waddington found another letter waiting for him on the breakfast-table.

Fanny was looking at him, and he sought protection in an affectation of annoyance.

"Now what can Mrs. Levitt find to write to me about?"

"I wouldn't set any limits to her invention," Fanny said.

"And what do you know about Mrs. Levitt?"

"Nothing. I only gather from what you say yourself that she is—fertile in resource."

"Resource?"

"Well, in creating opportunities."

"Opportunities, now, for what?"

"For you to exercise your Christian charity, my dear. When are you going to let me call on her?"

"I am not going to let you call on her at all."

"Is that Christian charity?"

"It's anything you please." He was absorbed in his letter. Mrs. Levitt had been obliged to move from Mrs. Trinder's in the Square to inferior rooms in Sheep Street, and she was sorry for herself.

"But surely, when you're always calling on her yourself—"

"I am not always calling on her. And if I were, there are some things which are perfectly proper for me to do which would not be proper for you."

"It sounds as if Mrs. Levitt wasn't."

He looked up as sharply as his facial curves permitted. "Nothing of the sort. She's simply not the sort of person you *do* call on; and I don't mean you to begin."

"Why not?"

"Because you're my wife and you have a certain position in the county. That's why."

"Rather a snobby reason, isn't it? You said I might call on anybody I liked."

"So you may, in reason, provided you don't begin with Mrs. Levitt."

"I may have to end with her," said Fanny.

Mr. Waddington had many reasons for not wishing Fanny to call on Mrs. Levitt. He wanted to keep his wife, because she was his wife, in a place apart from Mrs. Levitt and above her, to mark the distance and distinction that there was between them. He wanted to keep himself, as Fanny's husband, apart and distant, by way of enhancing his male attraction. And he wanted to keep Mrs. Levitt apart, to keep her to himself, as the hidden woman of passionate adventure. Hitherto their intercourse had had the charm, the unique, irreplaceable charm of things unacknowledged and clandestine. Mrs. Levitt was unique; irreplaceable. He couldn't think of any other woman who would be a suitable substitute. There was little Barbara Madden; she had been afraid of him; but his passions were still too young to be stirred by the crudity of a girl's fright; if it came to that, he preferred the reassuring ease of Mrs. Levitt.

And he didn't mean it to come to that.

But though Mr. Waddington did not actually look forward to a time when he would be Mrs. Levitt's lover, he had visions of the pure fancy in which he saw himself standing on Mrs. Levitt's doorstep after dark; say, once a fortnight, on her servant's night out; he would sound a muffled signal on the knocker and the door would he half-opened by Elise. Elise! He would slip through in a slender and mysterious manner; he would go on tip-toe up and down her stairs, recapturing a youthful thrill out of the very risks they ran, yet managing the affair with a consummate delicacy and discretion.

At this point Mr. Waddington's fancy heard another door open down the street; somebody came out and saw him in the light of the passage; somebody went by with a lantern; somebody timed his comings and goings. He felt the palpitation, the cold nausea of detection. No. You couldn't do these things in a little place like Wyck-on-the-Hill, where everybody knew everybody else's business. And there was Toby, too.

Sometimes, perhaps, on a Sunday afternoon, when Toby and the servant would be out. Yes. Sunday afternoon between tea-time and church-time.

Or he could meet her in Oxford or Cheltenham or in London. Wiser. Weekends. More satisfactory. Risk of being seen there too, but you must take some risks. Surprising how these things *were* kept secret.

Birmingham now. Birmingham would be safer because more unlikely. He didn't know anybody in Birmingham. But the very thought of Mrs. Levitt calling at the Manor on the same commonplace footing, say, as Mrs. Grainger, was destruction to all this romantic secrecy.

Also he was afraid that if Mrs. Levitt were really that sort of woman, Fanny's admirable instinct would find her out and scent the imminent affair. Or if Fanny remained unsuspicious and showed plainly her sense of security, Elise might become possessive and from sheer jealousy give herself away. Mr. Waddington said to himself that he knew women, and that if he were a wise man, and he *was* a wise man, he would arrange matters so that the two should never meet. Fanny was docile, and if he said flatly that she was not to call on Mrs. Levitt, she wouldn't.

2

There was another thing that Mr. Waddington dreaded even more than that dangerous encounter: Fanny's knowing that he had turned the Ballingers out. As he would have been very unwilling to admit that Mrs. Levitt had forced his hand there, he took the whole of the responsibility for that action. But, inevitable and justifiable as it was, he couldn't hope to carry it off triumphantly with Fanny. It was just, but it was not magnanimous. Therefore, without making any positively untruthful statement, he had let her think that Ballinger had given notice of his own accord. The chances, he thought, were all against Fanny ever hearing the truth of the matter.

If only the rascal hadn't had a wife and children, and if only his wife—but, unfortunately for Mr. Waddington, his wife was Susan Trinder, Mrs. Trinder's husband's niece, and Susan Trinder had been Horace's nurse; and though they all considered that she had done for herself when she married that pig-headed Ballinger, Fanny and Horace still called her Susan-Nanna. And Susan-Nanna's niece, Annie Trinder, was parlourmaid at the Manor. So Mr. Waddington had a nasty qualm when Annie, clearing away breakfast, asked if she might have a day off to look after her aunt, Mrs. Ballinger, who was in bed with the rheumatics.

To his horror he heard Fanny saying: "She wouldn't have had the rheumatics if they'd stayed in Sheep Street."

"No, ma'am."

Annie's eyes were clear and mendacious.

"He never ought to have left it," said Fanny.

"No, ma'am. No more he oughtn't."

"Isn't she very sorry about it?"

(Why couldn't Fanny leave it alone?)

"Yes, m'm. She's frettin' something awful. You see, 'tesn't so much the house, though 'tes a better one than the one they're in, 'tes the garden. All that fruit and vegetable what uncle he put in himself, and them lavender bushes. Aunt, she's so fond of a bit of lavender. I dunnow I'm sure how she'll get along."

Annie knew. He could tell by her eyes that she knew. There was nothing but Annie's loyalty between him and that exposure that he dreaded. He heard Fanny say that she would go and see Susan to-morrow. There would be nothing but Susan's loyalty and Ballinger's magnanimity. It would amount to that if they spared him for Fanny's sake. He had been absolutely right, and Ballinger had brought the whole trouble on himself; but you could never make Fanny see that. And Ballinger contrived to put him still further in the wrong. The next day when Fanny called at the cottage she found it empty. Ballinger had removed himself and his wife and family to Susan's father's farm at Medlicott, a good two and a half miles from his work on Colonel Grainger's land, thus providing himself with a genuine grievance.

And Fanny would keep on talking about it at dinner.

"Those poor Ballingers! It's an awful pity he gave up the Sheep Street cottage. Didn't you tell him he was a fool, Horatio?"

Mercifully Annie Trinder had left the room. But there was Partridge by the sideboard, listening.

"I'm not responsible for Ballinger's folly. If he finds himself inconvenienced by it, that's no concern of mine."

"Well, Ballinger's folly has been very convenient for Mrs. Levitt."

Mr. Waddington tried to look as if Mrs. Levitt's convenience were no concern of his either.

VII

1

The handbills and posters had been out for the last week. Their headlines were very delightful to the eye with their enormous capitals staring at you in Pyecraft's royal blue print.

NATIONAL LEAGUE OF LIBERTY.

* * * * *

A MEETING
IN AID OF THE ABOVE LEAGUE
WILL BE HELD IN THE
TOWN HALL, WYCK-ON-THE-HILL,
Saturday, June 21st, 8 p.m.

* * * * *

Chairman: SIR JOHN CORBETT,
OF
UNDERWOODS, WYCK-ON-THE-HILL.
Speaker:
HORATIO BYSSHE WADDINGTON, ESQ.,
OF THE
MANOR HOUSE, LOWER WYCK.

* * * * *

YOU ARE EARNESTLY REQUESTED TO ATTEND.

* * * * *

GOD SAVE THE KING!

Only one thing threatened Mr. Waddington's intense enjoyment of his meeting: his son Horace would be there. Young Horace had insisted on coming over from Cheltenham College for the night, expressly to attend the meeting. And though Mr. Waddington had pointed out that the meeting could very well take place without him, Fanny appeared to be backing young Horace up in his impudent opinion that it couldn't. This he found excessively annoying; for, though for worlds he wouldn't have owned it, Mr. Waddington was afraid of his son. He was never the same man when he was about. The presence of young Horace—tall for sixteen and developing rapidly—was fatal to the illusion of his youth. And Horace had a way of commenting disadvantageously on everything his father said or did; he had a perfect genius for humorous depreciation. At any rate, he and his mother behaved as if they thought it was humorous, and many of his remarks seemed to strike other people—Sir John and Lady Corbett, for example, and Ralph Bevan—in the same light. Over and over again young Horace would keep the whole table listening to him with unreasoning and unreasonable delight, while his father's efforts to converse received only a polite and perfunctory attention. And the prospect of having young Horace's humour let loose on his meeting and on his speech at the meeting was distinctly disagreeable. Fanny oughtn't to have allowed it to happen. He oughtn't to have allowed it himself. But short of writing to his Head Master to forbid it, they couldn't stop young Horace coming. He had only to get on his motor-bicycle and come.

Barbara came on him in the drawing-room before dinner, sitting in an easy chair and giggling over the prospectus.

He jumped up and stood by the hearth, smiling at her.

"I say, did my guv'nor really write this himself?"

"More or less. Did you really come over for the meeting?"

"Rather."

His smile was wilful and engaging.

"You *are* enthusiastic about the League."

"Enthusiastic? We-ell, I can't say I know much about it. Of course, I know the sort of putrid tosh he'll sling at them, but what I want is to *see* him doing it."

He had got it too, that passion of interest and amusement, hers and Ralph's. Only it wasn't decent of him to show it; she mustn't let him see she had it. She answered soberly:

"Yes, he's awfully keen."

"*Is* he? I've never seen him really excited, worked up, except once or twice during the war."

As he stood there, looking down, smiling pensively, he seemed to brood over it, to anticipate the joy of the spectacle.

He had an impudent, happy face, turned and coloured like his mother's; he had Fanny's blue eyes and brown hair. All that the Waddingtons and Postlethwaites had done to him was to raise the bridge of his nose, and to thicken his lips slightly without altering their wide, vivacious twirl. He considered Barbara.

"You're going to help him to write his book, aren't you?"

"I hope so," said Barbara.

"You've got a nerve. He pretty well did for Ralph Bevan. He's worse than shell-shock when he once gets going."

"I expect I can stand him. He can't be worse than the War Office."

"Oh, isn't he? You wait."

At that moment his father came in, late, and betraying the first symptoms of excitement. Barbara saw that the boy's eyes took them in. As they sat down to dinner Mr. Waddington pretended to ignore Horace. But Horace wouldn't be ignored. He drew attention instantly to himself.

"Don't you think it's jolly decent of me, pater, to come over for your meeting?"

"I shouldn't have thought," said Mr. Waddington, "that politics were much in your line. Not worth spoiling a half-holiday for."

"I don't suppose I shall care two fags about your old League. What I've come for is to see you, pater, getting up on your hind legs and giving it them. I wouldn't miss that for a million half-holidays."

"If that's all you've come for you might have saved yourself the trouble."

"Trouble? My dear father, I'd have taken *any* trouble."

You could see he was laughing at him. And he was talking at Barbara, attracting her attention the whole time; with every phrase he shot a look at her across the table. Evidently he was afraid she might think he didn't know how funny his father was, and he had to show her. It wasn't decent of him. Barbara didn't approve of young Horace; yet she couldn't resist him; his eyes and mouth were full, like Ralph's, of such intelligent yet irresponsible joy. He wanted her to share it. He was an egoist like his father; but he had something of his mother's charm, something of Ralph Bevan's.

"Nothing," he was saying, "nothing would have kept me away."

"You're very good, sir." Horace could appreciate that biting sarcasm.

"Not at all. I say, I wish you'd let me come on the platform."

"What for? You don't propose yourself as a speaker, do you?"

"Rather not. I simply want to be somewhere where I can see your face and old Grainger's at the same time, and Hitchin's, when you're going for their Socialism."

"You shall certainly not come on the platform. And wherever you sit I must request you to behave yourself—if you can. You may not realize it, but this is going to be a serious meeting."

"I know *that*. It's just the—the seriousness that gets me." He giggled.

Mr. Waddington shrugged his shoulders. "Of course, if you've no sense of responsibility—if you choose to go on like an ill-bred schoolboy—but don't be surprised if you're reprimanded from the chair."

"What? Old Corbett? I should like to see him.... Don't you worry, pater, I'll behave a jolly sight better than anybody else will. You see if I don't."

"How did you suppose he'd behave, Horatio?" said Fanny. "When he's come all that way and given up a picnic to hear you."

"Pater'll be a picnic, if you like," said Horace.

Mr. Waddington waved him away with a gesture as if he flicked a teasing fly, and went out to collect his papers.

Fanny turned to her son. "Horry dear, you mustn't rag your father like that. You mustn't laugh at him. He doesn't like it."

"I can't help it," Horry said. "He's so furiously funny. He *makes* me giggle."

"Well, whatever you do, don't giggle at the meeting, or you'll give him away."

"I won't, mater. Honour bright, I won't. I'll hold myself in like—like anything. Only you mustn't mind if I burst."

2

Mr. Waddington had spoken for half an hour, expounding, with some necessary repetitions, the principles and objects of the League.

He was supported on the platform by his Chairman, Sir John Corbett, and by the other members of his projected Committee: by Lady Corbett, by Fanny, by the Rector, by Mr. Thurston of the Elms, Wyck-on-the-Hill; by Mr. Bostock of Parson's Bank; Mr. Jackson, of Messrs. Jackson, Cleaver and Co., solicitors; Major Markham of Wyck Wold, Mr. Temple of Norton-in-Mark, and Mr. Hawtrey of Medlicott; and by his secretary, Miss Barbara Madden. The body of the hall was packed. Beneath him, in the front row, he had the wives and daughters of his committeemen; in its centre, right under his nose, he was painfully aware of the presence of young Horace and Ralph Bevan. Colonel Grainger sat behind them, conspicuous and, Mr. Waddington fancied, a little truculent, with his great square face and square-clipped red moustache, and on each side of Colonel Grainger and behind him were the neighbouring gentry and the townspeople of Wyck, the two grocers, the two butchers, the drapers and hotel keeper, and behind them again the servants of the Manor and a crowd of shop assistants; and further and further back, farm labourers and artisans; among these he recognized Ballinger with several of Colonel Grainger's and Hitchin's men. A pretty compact group they made, and Mr. Waddington was gratified by their appearance there.

And well in the centre of the hall, above the women's hats, he could see Mr. Hitchin's bush of hair, his shrewd, round, clean-shaven and rosy face, his grey check shoulders and red tie. Mr. Hitchin had the air of being supported by the entire body of his workmen. Mr. Waddington was gratified by Mr. Hitchin's appearance, too, and he thought he would insert some expression of that feeling in his peroration.

He was also profoundly aware of Mrs. Levitt sitting all by herself in an empty space about the middle of the third row.

From time to time Ralph Bevan and young Horace fixed on Fanny Waddington and Barbara delighted eyes in faces of a supernatural gravity. Young Horace was looking odd and unlike himself, with his jaws clamped together in his prodigious effort not to giggle. Whenever Barbara's eyes met his and Ralph's, a faint smile quivered on her face and flickered and went out.

Once Horace whispered to Ralph Bevan: "Isn't he going it?" And Ralph whispered back: "He's immense."

He was. He felt immense. He felt that he was carrying his audience with him. The sound of his own voice excited him and whipped him on. It was a sort of intoxication. He was soaring now, up and up, into his peroration.

"It is a gratification to me to see so many working men and women here to-night. They are specially welcome. We want to have them with us. Do not distrust the working man. The working man is sound at heart. Sound at head too, when he is let alone and not carried away by the treacherous arguments of ignorant agitators. We—myself and the founders of this League—have not that bad opinion of the working man which his leaders—his misleaders, I may call them—appear to have. We believe in him, we know that, if he were only let alone, there is no section of the community that would stand more solid for order and good government than he."

"Hear! Hear!" from Colonel Grainger. Ralph whispered, "Camouflage!" to Horace, who nodded.

"There is nothing in the aims of this League contrary to the interests of Labour. On the contrary"—he heard, as if somebody else had perpetrated it, the horrible repetition—"I mean to say—" His brain fought for another phrase madly and in vain. "On the contrary, it exists in order to safeguard the true interests, the best interests, of every working man and woman in the country."

"Hear! Hear!" from Sir John Corbett. Mr. Waddington smiled.

"President Wilson"—he became agitated and drank water—"President Wilson talked about making the world safe for democracy. Well, if we, you and I, all of us, don't take care, the world won't be safe for anything else. It certainly won't be safe for the middle classes, for the great business and professional classes, for the class to which I, for one, belong: the class of English gentlemen. It won't be safe for *us*.

"Not that I propose to make a class question of it. To make a class question of it would be more than wrong. It would be foolish. It would be a challenge to revolution, the first step towards letting loose, unchaining against us, those forces of disorder and destruction which we are seeking to keep down. I am not here to insist on class differences, to foment class hatred. Those differences exist, they always will exist; but they are immaterial to our big purpose. This is a question of principle, the great principle of British liberty. Are we going to submit to the tyranny of one class over all other classes, of one interest over all other interests in the country? Are we going to knock under, I say, to a minority, whether it is a Labour minority or any other?

"Are—we—going—to tolerate Bolshevism and a Soviet Government here? If there are any persons present who think that that is our attitude and our intention, I tell them now plainly—it is *not*. In their own language, in our good old county proverb: 'As sure as God's in Gloucester,' it is not and never will be. The sooner they understand that the better. I do not say that there are any persons present who would be guilty of so gross an error. I do not believe there are. I do not believe that there is any intelligent person in this room who will not agree with me when I say that, though it is just and right that Labour should have a voice in the government, it is not just and it is not right that it should be the only voice.

"It has been the only voice heard in Russia for two years, and what is the consequence? Bloodshed. Anarchy and bloodshed. I don't *say* that we should have anarchy and bloodshed here; England, thank God, is not Russia. But I do not say that we shall *not* have them. And I *do* say that it rests with us, with you and me, ladies and gentlemen, to decide whether we shall or shall not have them. It depends on the action we take to-night with regard to this National League of Liberty, on the action taken on—on other nights at similar meetings, all over this England of ours; it depends, in two words, on our *united action*, whether we shall have anarchy or stable government, whether this England of ours shall or shall not continue to be a free country.

"Remember two things: the League is National, and it is a League of Liberty. It would not be one if it were not the other.

"You will say, perhaps many of you *are* saying: 'This League is all very well, but what can *I* do?' Perhaps you will even say: 'What can Wyck do? After all, Wyck is a small place. It isn't the capital of the county.'"

"Well, I can tell you what Wyck can do. It can be—it *is* the first town in Gloucestershire, the first provincial town in England to start a National League of Liberty. They've got a League in London, the parent League; they may have another branch League anywhere any day, but I hope that—thanks to the very noble efforts of those ladies and gentlemen who have kindly consented to serve on my Committee—I hope that before long we shall have started Leagues in Gloucester, Cheltenham, Cirencester, Nailsworth and Stroud; in every town, village and hamlet in the county. I hope, thanks to your decision to-night, ladies and gentlemen, to be able to say that Wyck— little Wyck—has got in first. All round us, for fifteen—twenty miles round, there are hamlets, villages and towns that haven't got a League, that know nothing about the League. Wyck-on-the-Hill will be the centre of the League for this part of the Cotswolds.

"It is impossible to exaggerate the importance of the principle at stake. Impossible, therefore, to exaggerate the importance of this League, therefore impossible to exaggerate the importance of this meeting, of every man and woman who has come here to-night. And when you rise from your seats and step up to this platform to enroll your names as members of the National League of Liberty, I want you to feel, every one of you, that you will be doing an important thing, a thing necessary to the nation, a thing in its way every bit as necessary and important as the thing the soldier does when he rises up out of his trench and goes over the top."

It was then, and then only, that young Horace giggled. But he covered his collapse with a shout of "Hear! Hear!" that caused Fanny and Barbara to blow their noses simultaneously. As for Ralph, he hid his face in his hands.

"Like him," said Mr. Waddington, "you will be helping to save England. And what can any of us do more?"

He sat down suddenly in a perfect uproar of applause, and drank water. In spite of the applause he was haunted by a sense of incompleteness. There was something he had left out of his speech, something he had particularly wanted to say. It seemed to him more vital, more important, than anything he *had* said.

A solitary pair of hands, Mrs. Levitt's hands, conspicuously lifted, were still clapping when Mr. Hitchin's face rose like a red moon behind and a little to the left of her; followed by the grey check shoulders and red tie. He threw back his head, stuck a thumb in each armhole of his waistcoat, and spoke. "Ladies and gentlemen. The speaker has quoted President Wilson about the world being made safe for democracy. He seems to be concerned about the future, to be, if I may say so, in a bit of a funk about the future. But has he paid any attention to the past? Has he considered the position of the working man in the past? Has he even considered the condition of many working men at the present time, for instance, of the farm labourer now in this country? If he had, if he knew the facts, if he cared about the facts, he might admit that, whether he's going to like it or not, it's the working man's turn. Just about his turn.

"I needn't ask Mr. Waddington if he knows the parable of Dives and Lazarus. But I should like to say to him what Abraham said to the rich man: 'Remember that thou in thy life-time receivedst thy good things, and likewise Lazarus evil things: but now he is comforted and thou art tormented.'

"I don't want Mr. Waddington to be tormented. To be tormented too much. Not more than is reasonable. A little torment—say, his finger scorched for the fraction of a second in that hot, unpleasant place—would be good for him if it made him think. I say I don't want to torment him, but I'll just ask him one question: Does he think that a world where it's possible for a working man, just because he *is* a working man and not an English gentleman, a world where it's still possible for him, and his wife and his children, to be turned out of house and home to suit the whim of an English gentleman; does he think that a world where things like that can happen is a safe place for anybody?

"I can tell him it isn't safe. It isn't safe for you and me. And if it isn't safe for you and me, it isn't safe for the people who make these things happen; and it isn't any safer for the people who stand by and let them happen.

"And if the Socialist—if the Bolshevist is the man who's going to see to it that they don't happen, if a Soviet Government is the only Government that'll see to that, then the Socialist, or the Bolshevist, is the man for my money, and a Soviet Government is the Government for my vote. I don't say, mind you, that it *is* the only Government—I say, if it were.

"Mr. Waddington doesn't like Bolshevism. None of us like it. He doesn't like Socialism. I think he's got some wrong ideas about that. But he's dead right when he tells you, if you're afraid of Bolshevism and a Soviet Government, that the remedy lies in your own hands. If there ever is a day of reckoning, what Mr. Waddington would call a revolution in this country, you, we, ay, everyone of us sitting here, will be done with according as we do."

He sat down, and Mr. Waddington rose again on his platform, solemn and a little pale. He looked round the hall, to show that there was no person there whom he was afraid to face. It might have been the look of some bold and successful statesman turning on a turbulent House, confident in his power to hold it.

"Unless I have misheard him, what Mr. Hitchin has just said, ladies and gentlemen, sounded very like a threat. If that is so, we may congratulate Mr.

Hitchin on providing an unanswerable proof of the need for a National League of Liberty."

There were cries of "Hear! Hear!" from Sir John Corbett and from Mr. Hawtrey of Medlicott.

Then a horrible thing happened. Slight and rustling at first, then gathering volume, there came a hissing from the back rows packed with Colonel Grainger's and Mr. Hitchin's men. Then a booing. Then a booing and hissing together.

Sir John scrabbled on to his little legs and cried: "Ordah, there! Ordah!" Mr. Waddington maintained an indomitably supercilious air while Sir John brought his fist down on the table (probably the most energetic thing he had ever done in his life), with a loud shout of "Ordah!" Colonel Grainger and Mr. Hitchin were seen to turn round in their places and make a sign to their men, and the demonstration ceased.

Mr. Waddington then rose as if nothing at all had happened and said, "Any ladies and gentlemen wishing to join the League will please come up to the platform and give their names to Miss Madden. Any persons wishing to subscribe at once, may pay their subscriptions to Miss Madden.

"I will now call your attention to the last item on the programme, and ask you all to join with me very heartily in singing 'God Save the King.'"

Everybody, except Colonel Grainger and Mr. Hitchin, rose, and everybody, except the extremists of the opposition, sang. One voice—it was Mrs. Levitt's voice—was lifted arrogantly high and clear above the rest.

"Send—him—vic-torious,
Hap-py—and—glorious.
Long—to-oo rei-eign overious
Gaw-aw-awd—Save—ther King."

Mr. Waddington waited beside Barbara Madden at the table; he waited in a superb confidence. After all, the demonstration engineered by Colonel Grainger had had no effect. The front and middle rows had risen to their feet and a very considerable procession was beginning to file towards the platform.

Mr. Waddington was so intent on this procession, Barbara was so busy taking down names and entering subscriptions and making out receipts, Sir John and Lady Corbett and the rest of the proposed Committee were talking to each other so loud and fast, Ralph and Horace were so absorbed in looking at Barbara that none of them saw what was happening in the body of the hall. Only Fanny caught the signals that passed between Colonel Grainger and Mr. Hitchin, and between Mr. Hitchin and his men.

Then Colonel Grainger stood up and shouted, "I protest!"

Mr. Hitchin stood up and shouted, "I protest!"

They shouted together, "We protest!"

Sir John Corbett rushed back to his chair and shouted "Ordah!" and the back rows, the ranks of Hitchin's men, stood up and shouted, "We won't sign!" "We won't sign!" "We won't sign!"

And then young Horace did an unsuspected thing, a thing that surprised himself. He leaped on to the front bench and faced the insurgent back rows. His face was red with excitement, and with the shame and anger and resentment inspired by his father's eloquence. But he was shouting in his hoarse, breaking, adolescent voice:

"Look here, you blackguards there at the back. If you don't stop that row this minute, I'll jolly well chuck you all out."

Only one voice, the voice of Mr. Hitchin's biggest and brawniest quarryman, replied: "Come on, sir!"

Young Horace vaulted lightly over the bench, followed by Ralph, and the two were steeplechasing down the hall when Mr. Hitchin made another of his mysterious signals and the men filed out, obediently, one by one.

Ralph and Horace found themselves in the middle of the empty benches laughing into each other's faces. Colonel Grainger and Mr. Hitchin stood beside them, smiling with intolerable benevolence.

Mr. Hitchin was saying: "The men are all right, Mr. Bevan. They don't mean any harm. They just got a bit out of hand."

Horace saw that they were being magnanimous, and the thought maddened him. "I don't blame the men," he said, "and I don't blame you, Hitchin. You don't know any better. But Colonel Grainger ought to be damned well ashamed of himself, and I hope he is."

Colonel Grainger laughed. So did Mr. Hitchin, throwing himself back and swaying from side to side as his mirth shook him.

"Look here, Mr. Hitchin—"

"That'll do, Horry," said Ralph. He led him gently down a side aisle and through a swing door into the concealed corridor beside the platform. There they waited.

"Don't imagine for one moment," said young Horry, "that I agree with all that tosh he talked. But, after all, he's got a perfect right to make a fool of himself if he chooses. And he's *my* father."

"I know. From first to last, Horry, you behaved beautifully."

"Well, what would *you* do if your father made an unholy ass of himself in public?"

"My father doesn't."

"No, but if he did?"

"I'd do what you did. Sit tight and try and look as if he didn't."

"Then," said Horace, "you look as big a fool yourself."

"Not quite. You don't say anything. Besides, your father isn't as big a fool as those London Leaguers who started the silly show. Sir Maurice Gedge and all that crowd. He didn't invent the beastly thing."

"No," said Horace mournfully, "he hasn't even the merit of originality."

He meditated, still mournful.

"Look here, Ralph, what did that blackguard Hitchin mean?"

"He isn't a blackguard. He's a ripping good sort. I can tell you, if every employer in this confounded commercial country was as honest as old Hitchin, there wouldn't be any labour question worth talking about."

"Damn his honesty. What did he *mean*? Was it true what he said?"

"Was what true?"

"Why, that my father turned the Ballingers out?"

"Yes; I'm afraid it was."

"I say, how disgusting of him. You know I always thought he was a bit of a fool, my father; but I didn't know he was that beastly kind of fool."

"He isn't," said Ralph. "He's just—a fool."

"I know. Did you ever hear such putrid rot as he talked?"

"I don't know. For the kind of silly thing it was, his speech wasn't half bad."

"What? About going over the top? Oh, Lord! And after turning the Ballingers out, too."

Ralph was silent.

"What's happened to him? He didn't use to be like that. He must be mad, or something."

Ralph thought of Mrs. Levitt.

"He's getting old and he doesn't like it. That's what's the matter with him."

"But hang it all, Ralph, that's no excuse. It really isn't."

"I believe Ballinger gave him some provocation."

"I don't care what he gave him. He'd no earthly business to take advantage of it. Not with that sort of person. Besides, it wouldn't matter about Ballinger so much, but there's old Susan and the kiddies.... He doesn't see how perfectly sickening it is for *me*."

"It isn't very nice for your mother."

"No; it's jolly hard on the poor mater.... Well, I can't stick it much longer. I'm just about fed up with Horatio Bysshe. I shall clear out first thing in the morning before he's down. I don't care if I never see him or speak to him again."

"I say, I say, how about the midsummer holidays?"

"Oh, damn the midsummer holidays!"

"Isn't it rather rotten to take a line you can't possibly keep up?"

"That's all right. Whatever I may do in the future," said young Horace magnificently, "I've got to give him his punishment *now*."

Ralph laughed. Young Horace was as big an egoist as his father, but with these differences: his blood was hot instead of cold, he had his mother's humour, and he was not a fool. Ralph wondered how he would have felt if he had realized Mrs. Levitt's part in the Ballinger affair.

3

Mr. Waddington remained standing on his platform. They were coming round him now, grasping him by the hand, congratulating him: Sir John Corbett, the Rector, Major Markham of Wyck Wold and Mr. Hawtrey of Medlicott.

"Capital speech, Waddington, capital."

"Best speech made in the Town Hall since they built it."

"Splendid. You landed them one every time."

"No wonder you drew them down on to you."

"That was a disgraceful business," said Sir John. "Disgraceful."

"Nothing of the sort ever happened in Wyck before," said the Rector.

"Nobody ever made a speech like Waddington's before," said Major Markham of Wyck Wold.

"Oh, you always get a row if you drag in politics," Mr. Hawtrey said.

"I don't know," said Sir John. "That was a put-up job between Hitchin and Grainger."

"Struck me it had every appearance of a spontaneous outburst," Major Markham said.

"I've no doubt the rowdy element was brought in from the outside," said the Rector. "Hardly one of Hitchin's workpeople is a Wyck man. Otherwise I should have to apologize to Waddington for my parishioners."

"You needn't. There was nothing personal to me in it. Nothing personal at all. Even Hitchin wouldn't have had the impudence to oppose me on my own platform. It was the League they were going for. Bit too big for 'em. If you come out with a large, important thing like that there's sure to be some opposition just at first till it gets hold of 'em."

"Glad you can see it that way," said Sir John.

"My dear fellow, that's the way to see it. It's the right way; the big impersonal way."

"You've taken it in the proper spirit, Waddington," said the Rector. "None of those fellows meant any real harm. All good fellows.... By the way, is it true that the Ballingers have moved to Lower Wyck?"

"I believe so."

"Dear me, what on earth possessed them?"

"Some fad of Ballinger's, I fancy."

"That reminds me, I must go and see Mrs. Ballinger."

"You won't find them there, sir. They've moved again to her father's at Medlicott."

"You don't say so. I wonder now what they've done that for."

"They complained of the house being damp for one thing. If it was, that was Hitchin's fault, not mine."

Was everybody in a plot to badger him about those wretched Ballingers? He was getting sick of it. And he wanted to speak a word to Mrs. Levitt.

Mrs. Levitt had come up in the tail of the procession. She had given in her name and her subscription to Barbara Madden; but she lingered, waiting no doubt for a word with him. If only Corbett and the rest of them would go.

"Of course. Of course it was Hitchin's fault," said the Rector, with imperishable geniality. "Well.... Good night, Waddington, and thank you for a most—a most stimulating evening."

They had gone now, all but Sir John and Lady Corbett. (He could hear her talking to Fanny at the back of the platform.) Mrs. Levitt was gathering her scarf round her; in another minute she would be gone. And Corbett wouldn't go.

"I say, Waddington, that's a splendid young cub of yours. See him go over the top? He'd have taken them all on. Licked 'em, too, I shouldn't wonder."

Mr. Waddington resented this diversion of the stream of admiration. And he was acutely aware of Mrs. Levitt standing there, detached but waiting.

"Was I really all right, Corbett?" He wasn't satisfied with his speech. If only he could remember what he had left out of it.

"Absolutely, my dear chap. Absolutely top-hole. You ought to make that boy a soldier."

He wished that young Horace could be a soldier at that moment, stationed in a remote part of the Empire, without any likelihood of leave for the next five years. He wanted—he wanted intolerably to speak to Mrs. Levitt, to spread himself voluptuously in her rejuvenating smile.

Sir John retreated before his manifest indifference. He could hear him at the back of the platform, congratulating Fanny.

Mrs. Levitt advanced towards him.

"At last," she said, "I may add my congratulations. That speech was magnificent."

"Nothing, my dear lady, nothing but a little necessary plain speaking."

"Oh, but you were wonderful. You carried us off our feet."

"I hope," he said, "we've enrolled you as a member?" (He knew they had.)

"Of course I'm enrolled. And I've paid in my poor little guinea to that delightful Miss Madden."

"Ah, that is *too* good of you."

It was. The amount of the subscription was purely a matter of individual fancy.

"It's the least I could do in such a splendid cause."

"Well, dear Mrs. Levitt, we're delighted to have you with us. Delighted."

There was a pause. He was looking down at her from the height of his six feet. The faint, sweet scent of orris root rose up from her warm skin. She was very attractive, dressed in a low-necked gown of that dull, satiny stuff women were wearing now. A thin band of white net was stretched across the top of her breasts; through it he could see the shadowy, arrow-headed groove between; her pendant—pearl bistre and paste—pointed, pointed down to it.

He was wrong about Elise and jewellery. That was a throat for pearls and for diamonds. Emeralds. She would be all black and white and sparkling green. A necklace, he thought, wouldn't hang on her; it would be laid out, exposed on that white breast as on a cushion. You could never tell what a woman was really like till you'd seen her in a low-necked gown. It made Mrs. Levitt ten times more alluring. He smiled at her, a tender, brooding, rather fatuous smile.

Mrs. Levitt saw that her moment had come. It would be now or never. She must risk it.

"I wish," she said, "you'd introduce me to your wife."

It was a shock, a horrid blow. It showed plainly that Elise had interests beyond him, that she was not, like him, all for the secret, solitary adventure.

Yet perhaps—perhaps—she had planned it; she thought it would be safer for them, more discreet.

She looked up at him with the old, irrefutable smile.

"Will you?" she pleaded.

"Well—I'm not sure that I know where my wife *is*. She was here a minute ago, talking to Lady Corbett."

He looked round. A wide screen guarded the door on to the platform. He could see Lady Corbett and Fanny disappearing behind it.

"I—I'll go and look for her," he said. He meditated treachery. Treachery to poor Elise.

He followed them through the door and down the steps into the concealed corridor. He found Ralph Bevan there. Horace had gone.

"I say, Ralph, I wish you'd take Fanny home. She's tired. Get her out of this. I shall be here quite half an hour longer; settling up accounts. You might tell Kimber to come back for me and Miss Madden."

Now to get to the entrance you had to pass through the swing door into the hall and down the side aisle to the bottom, so that Mrs. Levitt witnessed Mrs. Waddington's exit with Ralph Bevan. Mr. Waddington. waited till the hall doors had closed on them before he returned.

"I can't find my wife anywhere," he said. "She wasn't in the cloak-room, so I think she must have gone back with Horace."

Mrs. Levitt would think that Fanny had disappeared while he was looking for her, honourably, in the cloak-room.

"I saw her go out," said Mrs. Levitt coldly, "with Mr. Bevan."

"I suppose he's taking her home," he said vaguely. His best policy was vagueness. "And now, my dear lady, I wish I could take *you* home. But I shall be detained here some little time. Still, if you don't mind waiting a minute or two till Kimber comes back with the car, he shall drive you."

"Thank you, Mr. Waddington, I'm afraid I've waited quite long enough. It isn't worth while troubling Kimber to drive me a hundred yards."

It gave her pleasure to inflict that snub on Mr. Waddington in return for his manoeuvre. As the meeting had now broken up, and there wouldn't be anybody to witness her departure in the Waddingtons' car, Mrs. Levitt calculated that she could afford that little gratification of her feelings. They were intensified by Mr. Waddington's very evident distress. He would have walked home with her the hundred yards to Sheep Street, but she wouldn't hear of it. She was perfectly capable of seeing herself home. Miss Madden was waiting for him. Good night.

4

Eleven o'clock. In the library where Mr. Waddington was drinking his whisky and water, Fanny had been crying. Horry had stalked off to his bedroom without saying good night to anybody. Barbara had retired discreetly. Ralph Bevan had gone. And when Fanny thought of the lavender bags Susan-Nanna sent every year at Christmas, she had cried.

"How could you *do* it, Horatio? How *could* you?"

"There was nothing else to be done. You can't expect me to take your sentimental, view of Ballinger."

"It isn't Ballinger. It's poor Susan-Nanna and the babies, and the lavender bags."

Mr. Waddington swayed placably up and down on the tips of his toes. "It serves poor Susan-Nanna right for marrying Ballinger."

"Oh—I suppose it serves *me* right, too—"

Though she clenched her hands tight, tight, she couldn't keep back that little spurt of anger.

He was smiling his peculiar, voluptuous smile. "Serves you right? For spoiling everybody in the village? It does indeed."

"You don't in the least see what I mean," said Fanny.

But, after all, she was glad he hadn't seen it.

He hadn't seen anything. He hadn't seen that she had been crying. It had never dawned on him that she might care about Susan-Nanna, or that the Ballingers might love their home, their garden and their lavender bushes. He was like that. He didn't see things, and he didn't care.

He was back in his triumph of the evening, going over the compliments and congratulations, again and again—"Best speech ever made in the Town Hall—" But there was something—something he had left out.

"Did it never dawn on you—" said Fanny.

Ah, *now* he had it.

"There!" he said. "I knew I'd forgotten something. I never put in that bit about the darkest hour before dawn."

Fanny's mind had wandered from what she had been going to say. "Did you see what Horry did?" she said instead.

"Everybody could see it. It was most unnecessary."

"I don't care. Think, Horatio. Think of his sticking up for you like that. He was going to fight them, the dear thing, all those great rough men. To fight them for *you.* He said he'd behave better than anybody else, and he did."

"Yes, yes. He behaved very well." Now that she put it to him that way he was touched by Horace's behaviour. He could always be touched by the thought of anything you did for *him.*

But Ralph Bevan could have told Fanny she was mistaken. Young Horace didn't do it altogether for his father; he did it for himself, for an ideal of conduct, an ideal of honour that he had, to let off steam, to make a sensation in the Town Hall, to feel himself magnificent and brave; because he, too, was an egoist, though a delightful one.

Mr. Waddington returned to his speech. "I can't think what made me leave out that bit about the dawn."

"Oh, bother your old dawn," said Fanny. "I'm going to bed."

She went, consoled. "Dear Horry," she thought, "I'm glad he did that."

VIII

1

The Ballinger affair did not end with the demonstration in the Town Hall. It had unforeseen and far-reaching consequences.

The first of these appeared in a letter which Mr. Waddington received from Mr. Hitchin:

"DEAR SIR,—

"*Re* my estimate for decoration and additional building to Mrs. Levitt's house, I beg to inform you that recent circumstances have rendered it impossible for me to take up the contract. I must therefore request you to transfer your esteemed order to some other firm.

"Faithfully yours,

"THOMAS HITCHIN."

Mr. Hitchin expressed his attitude even more clearly to the foreman of his works. "I'm not going to build bathrooms and boudoirs and bedrooms for that—" the word he chose completed the alliteration. So that Mr. Waddington was compelled to employ a Cheltenham builder whose estimate exceeded Mr. Hitchin's estimate by thirty pounds.

And Mr. Hitchin's refusal was felt, even by people who resented his estimates, to be a moral protest that did him credit. It impressed the popular imagination. In the popular imagination Mrs. Levitt was now inextricably mixed up with the Ballinger affair. Public sympathy was all with Ballinger, turned out of his house and forced to take refuge with his wife's father at Medlicott, forced to trudge two and a half miles every day to his work and back again. The Rector and Major Markham of Wyck Wold, meditating on the Ballinger affair as they walked back that night from the Town Hall, pronounced it a mystery.

"It wasn't likely," Major Markham said, "that Ballinger, of his own initiative, would leave a comfortable house in Sheep Street for a damp cottage in Lower Wyck."

"Was it likely," the Rector said, "that Waddington would turn him out?" He couldn't believe that old Waddington would do anything of the sort.

"Unless," Major Markham suggested, "he's been got at. Mrs. Levitt may have got at him." He was a good sort, old Waddy, but he would be very weak in the hands of a clever, unscrupulous woman.

The Rector said he thought there was no harm in Mrs. Levitt, and Major Markham replied that he didn't like the look of her.

A vague scandal rose in Wyck-on-the-Hill. It went from mouth to mouth in bar parlours and back shops; Major Markham transported it in his motor-car from Wyck Wold to the Halls and Manors of Winchway and Chipping Kingdon and Norton-in-Mark. It got an even firmer footing in the county than in Wyck, with the consequence that one old lady withdrew her subscription to the League, and that when Mr. Waddington started on his campaign of rounding up the county the county refused to be rounded up. And the big towns, Gloucester, Cheltenham and Cirencester, were singularly apathetic. It was intimated to Mr. Waddington that if the local authorities saw fit to take the matter up no doubt something would be done, but the big towns were not anxious for a National League of Liberty imposed on them from Wyck-on-the-Hill.

The League did not die of Mrs. Levitt all at once. Very soon after the inaugural meeting the Committee sat at Lower Wyck Manor and appointed Mr. Waddington president. It arranged a series of monthly meetings in the Town Hall at which Mr. Waddington would speak ("That," said Fanny, "will give you something to look forward to every month.") Thus, on Saturday, the nineteenth of July, he would speak on "The Truth about Bolshevism." It was also decided that the League could be made very useful during by-elections in the county, if there ever were any, and Mr. Waddington prepared in fancy a great speech which he could use for electioneering purposes.

On July the nineteenth, seventeen people, counting Fanny and Barbara, came to the meeting: Sir John Corbett (Lady Corbett was unfortunately unable to attend), the Rector without his wife, Major Markham of Wyck Wold, Mr. Bostock of Parson's Bank, Kimber and Partridge and Annie Trinder from the Manor, the landlady of the White Hart, the butcher, the grocer and the fishmonger with whom Mr. Waddington dealt, three farmers who approved of his determination to keep down wages, and Mrs. Levitt. When he sat down and drank water there was a feeble clapping led by Mrs. Levitt, Sir John and the Rector. On August the sixteenth, the audience had shrunk to Mrs. Levitt, Kimber and Partridge, the butcher, one of the three farmers, and a visitor staying at the White Hart. Mr. Waddington spoke on "What the League Can Do." Owing to a sudden unforeseen shortage in his ideas he was obliged to fall back on his electioneering speech and show how useful the League would be if at any time there were a by-election in the county. The pop-popping of Mrs. Levitt's hands burst into a silent space. Nobody, not even Kimber or Partridge, was going to follow Mrs. Levitt's lead.

"You'll have to give it up," Fanny said. "Next time there won't be anybody but Mrs. Levitt." And with the vision before him of all those foolish, empty benches and Mrs. Levitt, pop-popping, dear brave woman, all by herself, Mr. Waddington admitted that he would have to give it up. Not that he owned himself beaten; not that he gave up his opinion of the League.

"It's a bit too big for 'em," he said. "They can't grasp it. Sleepy minds. You can't rouse 'em if they won't be roused."

He emerged from his defeat with an unbroken sense of intellectual superiority.

2

Thus the League languished and died out; and Mr. Waddington, in the absence of this field for personal activity, languished too. In spite of his intellectual superiority, perhaps because of it, he languished till Barbara pointed out to him that the situation had its advantages. At last he could go on with his book.

"If you can only start him on it and keep him at it," Fanny said, "I'll bless you for ever."

But it was not easy either to start him or to keep him at it. To begin with, as Ralph had warned her, the work itself, *Ramblings Through the Cotswolds*, was in an appalling mess, and Mr. Waddington seemed to have exhausted his original impetus in getting it into that mess. He had set out on his ramblings without any settled plan. "A rambler," he said, "shouldn't have a settled plan." So that you would find Mr. Waddington, starting from Wyck-on-the-Hill and arriving at Lechford in the Thames valley, turning up in the valley of the Windlode or the Speed. You would find him on page twenty-seven drinking ale at the Lygon Arms in Chipping Kingdon, and on page twenty-eight looking down on the Evesham plain from the heights south of Cheltenham. He would turn from this prospect and, without traversing any intermediate ground, be back again, where you least expected him, in his Manor under Wyck-on-the-Hill. For though he had no fixed plan, he had a fixed idea, and however far he rambled he returned invariably to Wyck. To Mr. Waddington Wyck-on-the-Hill was the one stable, the one certain spot on the earth's surface, and this led to his treating the map of Gloucestershire entirely with reference to Wyck-on-the-Hill, so that all his ramblings were complicated by the necessity laid on him of starting from and getting back to it.

So much Barbara made out after she had copied the first forty pages, making the first clearing in Mr. Waddington's jungle. The clearings, she explained to Ralph, broke your heart. It wasn't till you'd got the thing all clean and tidy that you realized the deep spiritual confusion that lay behind it.

After that fortieth page the Ramblings piled and mixed themselves in three interpenetrating layers. First there was the original layer of Waddington, then a layer of Ralph superimposed on Waddington and striking down into him; then a top layer of Waddington, striking down into Ralph. First, the primeval chaos of Waddington; then Ralph's spirit moving over it and bringing in light and order; then Waddington again, invading it and beating it all back to darkness and confusion. From the moment Ralph came into it the progress of the book was a struggle between these two principles, and Waddington could never let Ralph be, so determined was he to stamp the book with his own personality.

"After all," Ralph said, "it *is* his book."

"If he could only get away from Wyck, so that you could see where the other places *are*," she moaned.

"He can't get away from it because he can't get away from himself. His mind is egocentric and his ego lives in Wyck."

Barbara had had to ask Ralph to help her. They were in the library together now, working on the Ramblings during one of Mr. Waddington's periodical flights to London.

"He thinks he's rambling round the country but he's really rambling round and round himself. All the time he's thinking about nothing but his blessed self."

"Oh, come, he thought a lot about his old League."

"No, the League was only an extension of his ego."

"That must have been what Fanny meant. We were looking at his portrait and I said I wondered what he was thinking about, and she said she used to wonder and now she knew. Of course, it's Himself. That's what makes him look so absurdly solemn."

"Yes, but think of it. Think. That man hasn't ever cared about anything or anybody but himself."

"Oh—he cares about Fanny."

"No. No, he doesn't. He cares about his wife. A very different thing."

"Well—he cares about his old mother. He really cares."

"Yes, and you know why? It's only because she makes him feel young. He hates Horry because he can't feel young when he's there."

"Why, oh why, did that angel Fanny marry him?"

"Because she isn't an angel. She's a mortal woman and she wanted a husband and children."

"Wasn't there anybody else?"

"I believe not—available. The man she ought to have married was married already."

"Did my mother marry him?"

"Yes. And *my* mother married the next best one.... It was as plain and simple as all that. And you see, the plainer and simpler it was, the more she realized why she was marrying Horatio, the more she idealized him. It wanted camouflage."

"I see."

"Then you must remember her people were badly off and he helped them. He was always doing things for them. He managed all Fanny's affairs for her before he married her."

"Then—he does kind things."

"Lots. When he wants to get something. He wanted to get Fanny.... Besides, he does them to get power, to get a hold on you. It's really for himself all the time. It gives him a certain simplicity and purity. He isn't a snob. He doesn't think about his money or his property, or his ancestors—he's got heaps— quite good ones. They don't matter. Nothing matters but himself."

"How about his book? Doesn't that matter?"

"It does and yet again it doesn't. He pretends he's only doing it to amuse himself, but it's really a projection of his ego into the Cotswolds. On the other hand, he'd hate it if you took him for a writing man when he's Horatio Bysshe Waddington. That's how he's got it into such a mess, because he can't get away from himself and his Manor."

"Proud of his Manor, anyhow."

"Oh, yes. Not, mind you, because it's perfect Tudor of the sixteenth century, *nor* because the Earl of Warwick gave it to his great-grandfather's great-great-grandfather, but because it's his Manor. Horatio Bysshe Waddington's Manor. Of course, it's got to be what it is because any other sort of Manor wouldn't be good enough for Bysshe."

"It's an extension of his ego, too?"

"Yes. Horatio's ego spreading itself in wings and bursting into ball-topped gables and overflowing into a lovely garden and a park. There isn't a tree, there isn't a flower that hasn't got bits of Horatio in it."

"If I thought that I should never want to see roses and larkspurs again."

"It only happens in Horatio's mind. But it does happen."

So, between them, bit by bit, they made him out.

And they made out the book. Here and there, on separate slips, were great outlying tracts of light, contributed by Ralph, to be inserted, and sketches of dark, undeveloped stuff, sprung from Waddington, to be inserted too. Neither Ralph nor Barbara could make them fit. The only thing was to copy it out clear as it stood and arrange it afterwards. And presently it appeared that two pages were missing.

One evening, the evening of Mr. Waddington's return, looking for the lost pages, Barbara made her great discovery: a sheaf of manuscript, a hundred and twenty pages in Ralph's handwriting, hidden away at the back of the bureau, crumpled as if an inimical hand had thrust it out of sight. She took it up to bed and read it there.

A hundred and twenty pages of pure Ralph without any taint of Waddington. It seemed to be part of Mr. Waddington's book, and yet no part of it, for it was inconceivable that it should belong to anything but itself. Ralph didn't ramble; he went straight for the things he had seen. He saw the Cotswolds round Wyck-on-the-Hill, he made you see them, as they were: the high curves of the hills, multiplied, thrown off, one after another; the squares and oblongs and vandykes and spread fans of the fields; and their many colours; grass green of the pastures, emerald green of the young wheat, white green of the barley; shining, metallic green of the turnips; the pink, the brown, the purple fallows, the sharp canary yellow of the charlock. And the trees, the long processions of trees by the great grass-bordered roads; trees furring the flanks and groins of the parted hills, dark combs topping their edges.

Ralph knew what he was doing. He went about with the farmers and farm hands; he followed the ploughing and sowing and the reaping, the feeding and milking of the cattle, the care of the ewes in labour and of the young lambs. He went at night to the upland folds with the shepherds; he could tell you about shepherds. He sat with the village women by their firesides and listened to their talk; he could tell you about village women. Mr. Waddington did not tell you about anything that mattered.

She took the manuscript to Ralph at the White Hart with a note to say how she had found it. He came running out to walk home with her.

"Did you know it was there?" she said.

"No. I thought I'd lost it. You see what it is?"

"Part of your book."

"Horatio's book."

"But you wrote it."

"Yes. That's what he fired me out for. He got tired of the thing and asked me to go on with it. He called it working up his material. I went on with it like that, and he wouldn't have it. He said it was badly written—jerky, short sentences—he'd have to re-write it. Well—I wouldn't let him do that, and he wouldn't have it as it stood."

"But—it's beautiful—alive and real. What more does he want?"

"The stamp of his personality."

"Oh, he'd *stamp* on it all right."

"I'm glad you like it."

"*Like* it. Don't you?"

Ralph said he thought he'd liked it when he wrote it, but now he didn't know.

"You'll know when you've finished it."

"I don't suppose I shall finish it," he said.

"But you must. You can't *not* finish a thing like that."

"I own I'd like to. But I can't publish it."

"Why ever not?"

"Oh, it wouldn't be fair to poor old Waddy. After all, I wrote it for him."

"What on earth does that matter? If he doesn't want it. Of course you'll finish it, and of course you'll publish it."

"Well, but it's all Cotswold, you see. And *he's* Cotswold. If it *is* any good, you know, I shouldn't like to—to well, get in his way. It's his game. At least he began it."

"It's a game two can play, writing Cotswold books."

"No. No. It isn't. And he got in first."

"Well, then, let him get in first. You can bring your book out after."

"And dish his?"

"No, let it have a run first. Perhaps it won't have any run."

"Perhaps mine won't."

"*Yours.* That heavenly book? And his tosh—Don't you see that you *can't* get in his way? If anybody reads him they won't be the same people who read you."

"I hope not. All the same it would be rather beastly to cut him out; I mean to come in and do it better, show how bad he is, how frightful. It would rub it in, you know."

"Not with him. You couldn't."

"You don't know. Some brute might get up and hurt him with it."

"Oh, you *are* tender to him."

"Well, you see, I did let him down when I left him. Besides, it isn't altogether him. There's Fanny."

"Fanny? She'd love you to write your book."

"I know she'd think she would. But she wouldn't like it if it made Horatio look a fool."

"But he's bound to look a fool in any case."

"True. I might give him a year, or two years."

"Well, then, *my* work's cut out for me. I shall have to make Horatio go on and finish quick, so as not to keep you waiting."

"He'll get sick of it. He'll make you go on with it."

"*Me?*"

"Practically, and quarrel with every word you write. Unless you can write so like Horatio that he'll think he's done it himself. And then, you know, he won't have a word of mine left in. You'll have to take me out. And we're so mixed up together that I don't believe even he could sort us. You see, in order to appease him, I got into the way of giving my sentences a Waddingtonian twist. If only I could have kept it up—"

"I'll have to lick the thing into shape somehow."

"There's only one thing you'll have to do. You must make him steer a proper course. This is to be *the* Guide to the Cotswolds. You can't have him sending people back to Lower Wyck Manor all the time. You'll have to know all the places and all the ways."

"And I don't."

"No. But I do. Supposing I took you on my motor-bike? Would you awfully mind sitting on the carrier?"

"Do you think," she said, "he'd let me go?"

"Fanny will."

"I *could*, I think. I work so hard in the mornings and evenings that they've given me all the afternoons."

"We might go every afternoon while the weather holds out," he said. And then: "I say, he *does* bring us together."

That was how Barbara's happy life began.

3

He did bring them together.

In the terrible months that followed, while she struggled for order and clarity against Mr. Waddington, who strove to reinstate himself in his obscure confusion, Barbara was sustained by the thought that in working for Mr. Waddington she was working for Ralph Bevan. The harder she worked for him the harder she worked for Ralph. With all her cunning and her little indomitable will she urged and drove him to get on and make way for Ralph. Mr. Waddington interposed all sorts of irritating obstructions and delays. He would sit for hours, brooding solemnly, equally unable to finish and to abandon any paragraph he had once begun. He had left the high roads and was rambling now in bye-ways of such intricacy that he was unable to give any clear account of himself. When Barbara had made a clean copy of it Mr. Waddington's part didn't always make sense. The only bits that could stand by themselves were Ralph's bits, and they were the bits that Mr. Waddington wouldn't let stand. The very clearness of the copy was a light flaring on the hopeless mess it was. Even Mr. Waddington could see it.

"Do you think," she said, "we've got it all down in the right order?" She pointed.

"*What's* that?" She could see his hands twitching with annoyance. His loose cheeks hung shaking as he brooded.

"That's not as *I*, wrote it," he said at last. "That's Ralph Bevan. He wasn't a bit of good to me. There's—there's no end to the harm he's done. Conceited fellow, full of himself and his own ideas. Now I shall have to go over every line he's written and write it again. I'd rather write a dozen books myself than patch up another fellow's bad work.... We've got to overhaul the whole thing and take out whatever he's done."

"But you're so mixed up you can't always tell."

He looked at her. "You may be sure that if any passage is obscure or confused or badly written it isn't mine. The one you've shown me, for example."

Then Barbara had another of her ideas. Since they were so mixed up together that Mr. Waddington couldn't tell which was which, and since he wanted to give the impression that Ralph was responsible for all the bad bits, and insisted on the complete elimination of Ralph, she had only got to eliminate the bad bits and give such a Waddingtonian turn to the good ones that he would be persuaded that he had written them himself.

The great thing was, he said, that the book should be written by himself. And once fairly extricated from his own entanglements and set going on a clear path, with Barbara to pull him out of all the awkward places, Mr. Waddington rambled along through the Cotswolds at a smooth, easy pace. Barbara had contrived to break him of his wasteful and expensive habit of returning from everywhere to Wyck. All through August he kept a steady course northeast, north, northwest; by September he had turned due south; he would be beating up east again by October; November would find him in the valleys; there was no reason why he shouldn't finish in December and come out in March.

Mr. Waddington himself was surprised at the progress he had made.

"It shows," he said, "what we can do without Ralph Bevan."

And Barbara, seated on Ralph's carrier, explored the countryside and mapped out Mr. Waddington's course for him.

"She's worth a dozen Ralph Bevins," he would say.

And he would go to the door with her and see her start.

"You mustn't let yourself be victimized by Ralph," he said. He glanced at the carrier. "Do you think it's safe?"

"Quite safe. If it isn't it'll only be a bit more thrilling."

"Much better to come in the car with me."

But Barbara wouldn't go in the car with him. When he talked about it she looked frightened and embarrassed.

Her fright and her embarrassment were delicious to Mr. Waddington. He said to himself: "She doesn't think *that's* safe, anyhow."

And as he watched her rushing away, swaying exquisitely over a series of terrific explosions, he gave a little skip and a half turn, light and youthful, in the porch of his Manor.

IX

1

Sir John Corbett had called in the morning. He had exerted himself to that extent out of friendship, pure friendship for Waddington, and he had chosen an early hour for his visit to mark it as a serious and extraordinary occasion. He sat now in the brown leather armchair which was twin to the one Mr. Waddington had sat in when he had his portrait painted. His jolly, rosy face was subdued to something serious and extraordinary. He had come to warn Mr. Waddington that scandal was beginning to attach itself to his acquaintance—he was going to say "relations," but remembered just in time that "relations" was a question-begging word—to his acquaintance with a certain lady.

To which Mr. Waddington replied, haughtily, that he had a perfect right to choose his—er—acquaintance. His acquaintance was, pre-eminently, his own affair.

"Quite so, my dear fellow, quite so. But, strictly between ourselves, is it a good thing to choose acquaintances of the sort that give rise to scandal? As a man of the world, now, between ourselves, doesn't it strike you that the lady in question may be that sort?"

"It does not strike me," said Mr. Waddington, "and I see no reason why it should strike you."

"I don't like the look of her," said Sir John, quoting Major Markham.

"If you're trying to suggest that she's not straight, you're reading something into her look that isn't there."

"Come, Waddington, you know as well as I do that when a man's knocked about the world like you and me, he gets an instinct; he can tell pretty well by looking at her whether a woman's that sort or not."

"My dear Corbett, my instinct is at least as good as yours. I've known Mrs. Levitt for three years, and I can assure she's as straight, as innocent, as your wife or mine."

"Clever—clever and a bit unscrupulous." Again Sir John quoted Major Markham. "A woman like that can get round simple fellows like you and me, Waddington, in no time, if she gives her mind to it. That's why I won't have anything to do with her. She may be as straight and innocent as you please; but somehow or other she's causing a great deal of unpleasant talk, and if I were you I'd drop her. Drop her."

"I shall do nothing of the sort."

"My dear fellow, that's all very well, but when everybody knows your wife hasn't called on her—"

"There was no need for Fanny to call on her. My relations with Mrs. Levitt were on a purely business footing—"

"Well, I'd leave them there, and not too much footing either."

"What can I do? Here she is, a war widow with nobody but me to look after her interests. She's got into the way of coming to me, and I'm not going back on the poor woman, Corbett, because of your absurd insinuations."

"Not *my* insinuations."

"Anybody's insinuations then. Nobody has a right to insinuate anything about *me*. As for Fanny, she'll make a point of calling on her now. We were talking about it not long ago."

"A bit hard on Mrs. Waddington to be let in for that."

"You needn't worry. Fanny can afford to do pretty well what she likes."

He had him there. Sir John knew that this was true of Fanny Waddington, as it was not true of Lady Corbett. He could remember the time when nobody called on his father and mother; and Lady Corbett could not, yet, afford to call on Mrs. Levitt before anybody else did.

"Well," he said, "so long as Mrs. Levitt doesn't expect my wife to follow suit."

"Mrs. Levitt's experience can't have led her to expect much in the way of kindness here."

"Well, don't be too kind. You don't know how you may be landed. You don't know," said Sir John fatally, "what ideas you may have put into the poor woman's head."

"I should be very sorry," said Mr. Waddington, "if I thought for one moment I had roused any warmer feelings—"

But he wasn't sorry. He tried hard to make his face express a chivalrous regret, and it wouldn't. It was positively smiling, so agreeable was the idea conveyed by Sir John. He turned it over and over, drawing out its delicious flavour, while Sir John's little laughing eyes observed his enjoyment.

"You don't know," he said, "*what* you may have roused."

There was something very irritating in his fat chuckle.

"You needn't disturb yourself. These things will happen. A woman may be carried away by her feelings, but if a man has any tact and any delicacy he can always show her very well—without breaking off all relations. That would be clumsy."

"Of course, if you want to keep up with her, keep up with her. Only take care you don't get landed, that's all."

"You may be quite sure that for the lady's own sake I shall take care."

They rose; Mr. Waddington stood looking down at Sir John and his little round stomach and his little round eyes with their obscene twinkle. And for the life of him he couldn't feel the indignation he would like to have felt. As his eyes encountered Sir John's something secret and primitive in Mr. Waddington responded to that obscene twinkle; something reminiscent and anticipating; something mischievous and subtle and delightful, subversive of dignity. It came up in his solemn face and simmered there. Here was Corbett, a thorough-paced man of the world, and he took it for granted that Mrs. Levitt's feelings had been roused; he acknowledged, handsomely, as male to male, the fascination that had roused them. He, Corbett, knew what he was talking about. He saw the whole possibility of romantic adventure with such flattering certitude that it was impossible to feel any resentment.

At the same time his interference was a piece of abominable impertinence, and Mr. Waddington resented that. It made him more than ever determined to pursue his relations with Mrs. Levitt, just to show he wasn't going to be dictated to, while the very fact that Corbett saw him as a figure of romantic adventure intensified the excitement of the pursuit. And though Elise, seen with certainty in the light of Corbett's intimations, was not quite so enthralling to the fancy as the Elise of his doubt, she made a more positive and formidable appeal to his desire. He loved his desire because it made him feel young, and, loving it, he thought he loved Elise.

And what Corbett was thinking, Markham and Thurston, and Hawtrey and young Hawtrey, and Grainger, would be thinking too. They would all see him as the still young, romantic adventurer, the inspirer of passion.

And Bevan—But no, he didn't want Bevan to see him like that. Or rather, he did, and yet again he didn't. He had scruples when it came to Bevan, because of Fanny. And because of Fanny, while he rioted in visions of the possible, he dreaded more than anything an actual detection, the raking eyes and furtive tongues of the townspeople. If Fanny called on Mrs. Levitt it would stop all the talking.

That was how Fanny came to know Mrs. Levitt, and how Mrs. Levitt (and Toby) came to be asked to the September garden party at Lower Wyck Manor.

2

Mrs. Levitt, of the White House, Wyck-on-the-Hill, Gloucestershire.

She thought it sounded very well. She had been out, that is to say, she had judged it more becoming to her dignity not to be at home when Fanny called; and Fanny had been actually out when Mrs. Levitt called, so that they met for the first time at the garden party.

"It's absurd our not knowing each other," Fanny said, "when my husband knows you so well."

"I've always felt, Mrs. Waddington, that I ought to know you, if it's only to tell you how good he's been to me. But, of course, you know it."

"I know it quite well. He's always being good to people. He likes it. You must take off some of the credit for that."

She thought: "She has really very beautiful eyes." A lot of credit would have to be taken off for her eyes, too.

"But isn't that," said Mrs. Levitt, "what being good *is*? To like being it? Only I suppose that's just what lays him open—"

She lowered the eyes whose brilliance had blazed a moment ago on Fanny; she toyed with her handbag, smiling a little secret, roguish smile.

"That lays him open?"

Mrs. Levitt looked up, smiling. "To the attacks of unscrupulous people like me."

It was risky, but it showed a masterly boldness and presence of mind. It was as if she and Fanny Waddington had had their eyes fixed on a live scorpion approaching them over the lawn, and Mrs. Levitt had stooped down and grasped it by its tail and tossed it into the lavender bushes. As if Mrs. Levitt had said, "My dear Mrs. Waddington, we both know that this horrible creature exists, but we aren't going to let it sting us." As if she knew why Fanny had called on her and was grateful to her.

Perhaps if Mrs. Levitt had never appeared at that garden party, or if, having appeared, she had never been introduced, at their own request, to Major Markham, Mr. Thurston, Mr. Hawtrey and young Hawtrey and Sir John Corbett, Mr. Waddington might never have realized the full extent of her fascination.

She had made herself the centre of the party by her sheer power to seize attention and to hold it. You couldn't help looking at her, again and again, where she sat in a clearing of the lawn, playing the clever, pointed play of her black and white, black satin frock, black satin cloak lined with white silk, furred with ermine; white stockings and long white gloves, the close black satin hat clipping her head; the vivid contrast and stress repeated in white skin, black hair, black eyes; black eyes and fine mouth and white teeth making a charming and perpetual movement.

She had been talking to Major Markham for the last ten minutes, displaying herself as the absurdly youthful mother of a grown-up son. Toby Levitt, a tall and slender likeness of his mother, was playing tennis with distinction, ignoring young Horace, his partner, standing well up to the net and repeating the alternate smashing and sliding strokes that kept Ralph and Barbara bounding from one end of the court to the other. Mrs. Levitt was trying to reconcile the proficiency of Toby's play with his immunity from conscription in the late war. The war led straight to Major Markham's battery, and Major Markham's battery to the battery once commanded by Toby's father, which led to Poona and the great discovery.

"You don't mean Frank Levitt, captain in the gunners?"

"I do."

"Was he by any chance stationed at Poona in nineteen-ten, eleven?"

"He was."

"But, bless my soul—*he* was my brother-in-law Dick—Dick Benham's best friend."

The Major's slightly ironical homage had given place to a serious excitement, a respectful interest.

"Oh—Dicky Benham—is *he*—?"

"Rather. I've heard him talk about Frank Levitt scores of times. Do you hear that, Waddington? Mrs. Levitt knows all my sister's people. Why on earth haven't we met before?"

Mr. Waddington writhed, while between them they reeled off a long series of names, people and places, each a link joining up Major Markham and Mrs. Levitt. The Major was so excited about it that he went round the garden telling Thurston and Hawtrey and Corbett, so that presently all these gentlemen formed round Mrs. Levitt an interested and animated group. Mr. Waddington hovered miserably on the edge of it; short of thrusting Markham aside with his elbow (Markham for choice) he couldn't have broken through. He would give it up and go away, and be drawn back again and again; but though Mrs. Levitt could see him plainly, no summons from her beautiful eyes invited his approach.

His behaviour became noticeable. It was observed chiefly by his son Horry.

Horry took Barbara apart. "I say, have you seen my guv'nor?"

"No. What? Where?"

She could see by his face that he was drawing her into some iniquitous, secret by-path of diversion.

"There, just behind you. Turn round—this way—but don't look as if you'd spotted him.... Did you ever see anything like him? He's like a Newfoundland dog trying to look over a gate. It wouldn't be half so funny if he wasn't so dignified all the time."

She didn't approve of Horry. He wasn't decent. But the dignity—it *was* wonderful.

Horry went on. "What on earth did the mater ask that woman for? She might have known he'd make a fool of himself."

"Oh, Horry, you mustn't. It's awful of you. You really *are* a little beast."

"I'm not. Fancy doing it at his own garden party. He never thinks of *us*. Look at the dear little mater, there, pretending she doesn't see him. *That's* what makes me mad, Barbara."

"Well, you ought to pretend you don't see it, too."

"I've been pretending the whole blessed afternoon. But it's no good pretending with *you*. You jolly well see everything."

"I don't go and draw other people's attention to it."

"Oh, come, how about Ralph? You know you wouldn't let him miss him."

"Ralph? Oh, Ralph's different. I shouldn't point him out to Lady Corbett."

"No more should I. *You're* different, too. You and Ralph and me are the only people capable of appreciating him. Though I wouldn't swear that the mater doesn't, sometimes."

"Yes. But you go too far, Horry. You're cruel to him, and we're not."

"It's all very well for you. He isn't your father.... Oh, Lord, he's craning his neck over Markham's shoulder now. What his face must look like from the other side—"

"If you found your father drunk under a lilac bush I believe you'd go and fetch me to look at him."

"I would, if he was as funny as he is now.... But I say, you know, I can't have him going on like that. I've got to stop it, somehow. What would you do if you were me?"

"Do? I think I should ask him to go and take Lady Corbett in to tea."

"Good."

Horry strode up to his father. "I say, pater, aren't you going to take Lady Corbett in to tea?"

At the sheer sound of his son's voice Mr. Waddington's dignity stood firm. But he went off to find Lady Corbett all the same.

When it was all over the garden party was pronounced a great success, and Mr. Waddington was very agreeably rallied on his discovery, taxed with trying to keep it to himself, and warned that, he wasn't going to have it all his own way.

"It's our turn now," said Major Markham, "to have a look in."

And their turn was constantly coming round again; they were always looking in at the White House. First, Major Markham called. Then Sir John Corbett of Underwoods, Mr. Thurston of The Elms, and Mr. Hawtrey of Medlicott called and brought their wives. These ladies, however, didn't like Mrs. Levitt, and they were not at home when she returned their calls. Mrs. Levitt's visiting card had its place in three collections and there the matter ended. But Mr. Thurston and Mr. Hawtrey continued to call with a delightful sense of doing something that their wives considered improper. Major Markham—as a bachelor his movements were more untrammelled—declared it his ambition to "cut Waddy out." *He* was everlastingly calling at the White House. His fastidious correctness, the correctness that hadn't "liked the look of her," excused this intensive culture of Mrs. Levitt on the grounds that she was "well connected"; she knew all his sister's people.

And Mrs. Levitt took good care to let Mr. Waddington know of these visits, and of her little bridge parties in the evening. "Just Mr. Thurston and Mr. Hawtrey and Major Markham and me." He was teased and worried by his visions of Elise perpetually surrounded by Thurston and Hawtrey and the Major. Supposing—only supposing that—driven by despair, of course—she married that fellow Markham? For the first time in his life Mr. Waddington experienced jealousy. Elise had ceased to be the subject of dreamy, doubtful speculation and had become the object of an uneasy passion. He could give her passion, if it was passion that she wanted; but, because of Fanny, he could not give her a position in the county, and it was just possible that Elise might prefer a position.

And Elise was happy, happy in her communion with Mr. Thurston and Mr. Hawtrey and in the thought that their wives detested her; happy in her increasing intimacy with Major Markham and in her consciousness of being well connected; above all, happy in Mr. Waddington's uneasiness.

Meanwhile Fanny Waddington kept on calling. "If I don't," she said, "the poor woman will be done for."

She couldn't see any harm in Mrs. Levitt.

3

Barbara and Ralph Bevan had been for one of their long walks. They were coming back down the Park when they met, first, Henry, the gardener's boy, carrying a basket of fat, golden pears.

"Where are you going with those lovely pears, Henry?"

"Mrs. Levitt's, miss." The boy grinned and twinkled; you could almost have fancied that he knew.

Farther on, near the white gate, they could see Mr. Waddington and two ladies. He had evidently gone out to open the gate, and was walking on with them, unable to tear himself away. The ladies were Mrs. Rickards and Mrs. Levitt.

They stopped. You could see the flutter of their hands and faces, suggesting a final triangular exchange of playfulness.

Then Mr. Waddington, executing a complicated movement of farewell, a bow and a half turn, a gambolling skip, the gesture of his ungovernable youth.

Then, as he went from them, the abandonment of Mrs. Rickards and Mrs. Levitt to disgraceful laughter.

Mrs. Levitt clutched her sister's arm and clung to it, almost perceptibly reeling, as if she said: "Hold me up or I shall collapse. It's too much. Too—too—too—too much." They came on with a peculiar rolling, helpless walk, rocked by the intolerable explosions of their mirth, dabbing their mouths and eyes with their pocket-handkerchiefs in a tortured struggle for control.

They recovered sufficiently to pass Ralph and Barbara with serious, sidelong bows. And then there was a sound, a thin, wheezing, soaring yet stifled sound, the cry of a conquered hysteria.

"Did you see that, Ralph?"

"I did. I heard it."

"*He* couldn't, could he?"

"Oh, Lord, no…. They appreciate him, too, Barbara."

"That isn't the way," she said. "We don't want him appreciated that way. That rich, gross way."

- 82 -

"No. It isn't nearly subtle enough. Any fool could see that his caracoling was funny. They don't know him as we know him. They don't know what he really is."

"It was an outrage. It's like taking a fine thing and vulgarizing it. They'd no *business.* And it was cruel, too, to laugh at him like that before his back was turned. When they're going to eat his pears, too."

"The fact is, Barbara, nobody *does* appreciate him as you and I do."

"Horry?"

"No. Not Horry. He goes too far. Horry's indecent. Fanny, perhaps, sometimes."

"Fanny doesn't see one half of him. She doesn't see his Mrs. Levitt side."

"Have *you* seen it, Barbara?"

"Of course I have."

"You never told me. It isn't fair to go discovering things on your own and not telling me. We must make a compact. To tell each other the very instant we see a thing. We might keep count and give points to which of us sees most. Mrs. Levitt ought to have been a hundred to your score."

"I'm afraid I can't score with Mrs. Levitt. You saw that, too."

"It'll be a game for gods, Barbara."

"But, Ralph, there might be things we *couldn't* tell each other. It mightn't be fair to him."

"Telling each other isn't like telling other people. Hang it all, if we're making a study of him we're making a study. Science is science. We've no right to suppress anything. At any moment one of us might see something absolutely vital."

"Whatever we do we musn't be unfair to him."

"But he's ours, isn't he? We can't be unfair to him. And we've got to be fair to each other. Think of the frightful advantage you might have over me. You're bound to see more things than I do."

"I might see more, but you'll understand more."

"Well, then, you can't do without me. It's a compact, isn't it, that we don't keep things back?"

As for Mrs. Levitt's handling of their theme they resented it as an abominable profanation.

"Do you think he's in love with her?" Barbara said.

"What *he* would call being in love and we shouldn't."

"Do you think he's like that—he's always been like that?"

"I think he was probably 'like that' when he was young."

"Before he married Fanny?"

"Before he married Fanny."

"And after?"

"After, I should imagine he went pretty straight. It was only the way he had when he was young. Now he's middle-aged he's gone back to it, just to prove to himself that he's young still. I take it the poor old thing got scared when he found himself past fifty, and he *had* to start a proof. It's his egoism all over again. I don't suppose he really cares a rap for Mrs. Levitt."

"You don't think his heart beats faster when he sees her coming?"

"I don't. Horatio's heart beats faster when he sees himself making love to her."

"I see. It's just middle age."

"Just middle age."

"Don't you think, perhaps, Fanny does see it?"

"No. Not that. Not that. At least I hope not."

X

Mr. Waddington's *Ramblings Through the Cotswolds* were to be profusely illustrated. The question was: photographs or original drawings? And he had decided, after much consideration, on photographs taken by Pyecraft's man. For a book of such capital importance the work of an inferior or obscure illustrator was not to be thought of for an instant. But there were grave disadvantages in employing a distinguished artist. It would entail not only heavy expenses, but a disastrous rivalry. The illustrations, so far from drawing attention to the text and fixing it firmly there, would inevitably distract it. And the artist's celebrated name would have to figure conspicuously, in exact proportion to his celebrity, on the title page and in all the reviews and advertisements where, properly speaking, Horatio Bysshe Waddington should stand alone. It was even possible, as Fanny very intelligently pointed out, that a sufficiently distinguished illustrator might succeed in capturing the enthusiasm of the critics to the utter extinction of the author, who might consider himself lucky if he was mentioned at all.

But Fanny had shown rather less intelligence in using this argument to support her suggestion that Barbara Madden should illustrate the book. She had more than once come upon the child, sitting on a camp-stool above Mrs. Levitt's house, making a sketch of the steep street, all cream white and pink and grey, opening out on to the many-coloured fields and the blue eastern air. And she had conceived a preposterous admiration for Barbara Madden's work.

"It'll be an enchanting book if she illustrates it, Horatio."

"*If* she illustrates it!"

But when he tried to show Fanny the absurdity of the idea—Horatio Bysshe Waddington illustrated by Barbara Madden—she laughed in his face and told him he was a conceited old thing. To which he replied, with dignified self-restraint, that he was writing a serious and important book. It would be foolish to pretend that it was not serious and important. He hoped he had no overweening opinion of its merits, but one must preserve some sense of proportion and propriety—some sanity.

"Poor little Barbara!"

"It isn't poor little Barbara's book, my dear."

"No," said Fanny. "It isn't."

Meanwhile, if the book was to be ready for publication in the spring, the photographs would have to be taken at once, before the light and the leaves were gone.

So Pyecraft and Pyecraft's man came with their best camera, and photographed and photographed, as long as the fine weather lasted. They photographed the Market Square, Wyck-on-the-Hill; they photographed the church; they photographed Lower Wyck village and the Manor House, the residence—corrected to seat—of Mr. Horatio Bysshe Waddington, the author. They photographed the Tudor porch, showing the figures of the author and of Mrs. Waddington, his wife, and Miss Barbara Madden, his secretary. They photographed the author sitting in his garden; they photographed him in his park, mounted on his mare, Speedwell; and they photographed him in his motor-car. Then they came in and looked at the library and photographed that, with Mr. Waddington sitting in it at his writing-table.

"I suppose, sir," Mr. Pyecraft said, "you'd wish it taken from one end to show the proportions?"

"Certainly," said Mr. Waddington.

And when Pyecraft came the next day with the proofs he said, "I think, sir, we've got the proportions very well."

Mr. Waddington stared at the proofs, holding them in a hand that trembled slightly with emotion. With a just annoyance. For though Pyecraft had certainly got the proportions of the library, Mr. Waddington's head was reduced to a mere black spot in the far corner.

If *that* was what Pyecraft meant by proportion—

"I think," he said, "the—er—the figure is not quite satisfactory."

"The—? I see, sir. I did not understand, sir, that you wished the figure."

"We-ell—" Mr. Waddington didn't like to appear as having wished the figure so ardently as he did indeed wish it. "If I'm to be there at all—"

"Quite so, sir. But if you wish the size of the library to be shown, I am afraid the figure must be sacrificed. We can't do you it both ways. But how would you think, sir, of being photographed yourself, somewhat larger, seated at your writing-table? We could do you that."

"I hadn't thought of it, Pyecraft."

As a matter of fact, he had thought of nothing else. He had the title of the picture in his mind: "The Author at Work in the Library, Lower Wyck Manor."

Pyecraft waited in deference to Mr. Waddington's hesitation. His man, less delicate but more discerning, was already preparing to adjust the camera.

Mr. Waddington turned, like a man torn between personal distaste and public duty, to Barbara.

"What do *you* think, Miss Madden?"

"I think the book would hardly be complete without you."

"Very well. You hear, Pyecraft, Miss Madden says I am to be photographed."

"Very good, sir."

He wheeled sportively. "Now how am I to sit?"

"If you would set yourself so, sir. With your papers before you, spread careless, so. And your pen in your hand, so.... A little nearer, Bateman. The figure is important this time.... *Now*, sir, if you would be so good as to look up."

Mr. Waddington looked up with a face of such extraordinary solemnity that Mr. Pyecraft smiled in spite of his deference.

"A leetle brighter expression. As if you had just got an idea."

Mr. Waddington imagined himself getting an idea and tried to look like it.

"Perfect—perfect." Mr. Pyecraft almost danced with excitement. "Keep that look on your face, sir, half a moment.... Now, Bateman."

A click.

"*That's* over, thank goodness," said Mr. Waddington, reluctant victim of Pyecraft's and Barbara's importunity.

After that Mr. Pyecraft and his man were driven about the country taking photographs. In one of them Mr. Waddington appeared standing outside the mediaeval Market Hall of Chipping Kingdon. In another, wearing fishing boots, and holding a fishing-rod in his hand, he waded knee deep in the trout stream between Upper and Lower Speed.

And after that he said firmly, "I will not be photographed any more. They've got enough of me."

2

In November, when the photographing was done, Fanny went away to London for a fortnight, leaving Barbara, as she said, to take care of Horatio, and Ralph Bevan to take care of Barbara.

It was then, in consequence of letters he received from Mrs. Levitt, that Mr. Waddington's visits in Sheep Street became noticeably frequent. Barbara, sitting on her camp-stool above the White House, noticed them.

She noticed, too, the singular abstraction of Mr. Waddington's manner in these days. There were even moments when he ceased to take any interest in his Ramblings, and left Barbara to continue them, as Ralph had continued them, alone, reserving to himself the authority of supervision. She had long stretches of time to herself, when she had reason to suspect that Mr. Waddington was driving Mrs. Leavitt to Cheltenham or Stratford-on-Avon in his car, while Ralph Bevan obeyed Fanny's parting charge to look after Barbara.

Every time Barbara did a piece of the Ramblings she showed it to Ralph Bevan. They would ride off together into the open country, and Barbara would read aloud to Ralph, sitting by the roadside where they lunched, or in some inn parlour where they had tea. They had decided that, though it would be dishonourable of Barbara to show him the bits that Mr. Waddington had written, there could be no earthly harm in trusting him with the bits she had done herself.

Not that you could tell the difference. Barbara had worked hard, knowing that the sooner Mr. Waddington's book was finished the sooner Ralph's book would come out; and under this agreeable stimulus she had developed into the perfect parodist of Waddington. She had wallowed in Waddington's style till she was saturated with it and wrote automatically about "bold escarpments" and "the rosy flush on the high forehead of Cleeve Cloud"; about "ivy-mantled houses resting in the shade of immemorial elms"; about the vale of the Windlode, "awash with the golden light of even," and "grey villages nestling in the beech-clad hollows of the hills."

"'Come with me,'" said Barbara, "'into the little sheltered valley of the Speed; let us follow the brown trout stream that goes purling—'"

"Barbara, it's priceless. What made you think of purling?"

"*He'd* have thought of it. 'Purling through the lush green grass of the meadows.'"

Or, "'Let us away along the great high road that runs across the uplands that divide the valleys of the Windlode and the Thames. Let us rest a moment halfway and drink—no, quaff—a mug of good Gloucestershire ale with mine host of the Merry Mouth.'"

Not that Mr. Waddington had ever done such a thing in his life. But all the other ramblers through the Cotswolds did it, or said they did it; and he was saturated with their spirit, as Barbara was saturated with his. He could see them, robust and genial young men in tweed knickerbocker suits, tramping their thirty miles a day and quaffing mugs of ale in every tavern; and he desired to present himself, like those young men, as genial and robust. He couldn't get away from them and their books any more than he had got away from Sir Maurice Gedge and his prospectus.

And Barbara had invented all sorts of robust and genial things for him to do. She dressed him in pink, and mounted him on his mare Speedwell, and sent him flying over the stone walls and five-barred gates to the baying of "Ranter and Ranger and Bellman and True." He fished and he tramped and he quaffed and he tramped again. He did his thirty miles a day easily. She set down long conversations between Mr. Waddington and old Billy, the Cotswold shepherd, all about the good old Cotswold ways, in the good old days when the good old Squire, Mr. Waddington's father—no, his grandfather—was alive.

"'I do call to mind, zur, what old Squire did use to zay to me: "Billy," 'e zays, "your grandchildren won't be fed, nor they won't 'ave the cottages, nor yet the clothes as you 'ave and your children. As zure as God's in Gloucester" 'e zays. They was rare old times, zur, and they be gawn.'"

"*What* made you think of it, Barbara? I don't suppose he ever said two words to old Billy in his life."

"Of course he didn't. 'But it's the sort of thing he'd like to think he did."

"Has he passed it?"

"Rather. He's as pleased as Punch. He thinks he's forming my style."

3

Mr. Waddington was rapidly acquiring the habit of going round to Sheep Street after dinner. But in those evenings that he did not devote to Mrs. Levitt he applied himself to his task of supervision.

On the whole he was delighted with his secretary. There could be no doubt that the little thing was deeply attached to him. You could tell that by the way she worked, by her ardour and eagerness to please him. There could be only one explanation of the ease with which she had received the stamp of his personality.

Therefore he used tact. He used tact.

"I'm giving you a great deal of work, Barbara," he would say. "But you must look on it as part of your training. You're learning to write good English. There's nothing like clear, easy, flowing sentences. You can't have literature without 'em. I might have written those passages myself. In fact, I can hardly distinguish—" His face shook over it; she noticed the tremor of imminent revision. "Still, I *think* I should prefer 'babbling streams' here to 'purling streams.' Shakespearean."

"I *had* 'babbling' first," said Barbara, "but I thought 'purling' would be nearer to what you'd have written yourself. I forgot about Shakespeare. And babbling isn't exactly purling, is it?"

"True—true. Babbling is *not* purling. We want the exact word. Purling let it be....

"And 'lush.' Good girl. You remembered that 'lush' was one of my words?"

"I thought it *would* be."

"Good. You see," said Mr. Waddington, "how you learn. You're getting the sense, the *flair* for style. I shall always be glad to think I trained you, Barbara.... And you may be very thankful it *is* I and not Ralph Bevan. Of all the jerky—eccentric—incoherent—"

XI

1

It was Monday, the twenty-fourth day of November, in the last week of Fanny's fortnight in London.

Barbara had been busy all morning with Mr. Waddington's correspondence and accounts. And now, for the first time, she found herself definitely on the track of Mrs. Levitt. In checking Palmer and Hoskins's, the Cheltenham builders, bill for the White House she had come across two substantial items not included in their original estimate: no less than fifteen by eight feet of trellis for the garden and a hot water pipe rail for the bathroom. It turned out that Mrs. Levitt, desiring the comfort of hot towels, and objecting to the view of the kitchen yard as seen from the lawn, had incontinently ordered the hot water rail and the trellis.

There was that letter from Messrs. Jackson and Cleaver, Mr. Waddington's agents, informing him that his tenant, Mrs. Levitt, of the White House, Wyck-on-the-Hill, had not yet paid her rent due on the twenty-fifth of September. Did Mr. Waddington wish them to apply again?

And there were other letters of which Barbara was requested to make copies from his dictation. Thus:

"My Dear Mrs. Levitt" (only he had written "My dear Elise"),—"With reference to your investments I do not recommend the purchase, at the present moment, of Government Housing Bonds.

"I shall be very glad to loan you the fifty pounds you require to make up the five hundred for the purchase of Parson's Provincial and London Bank Shares. But I am afraid I cannot definitely promise an advance of five hundred on the securities you name. That promise was conditional, and you must give me a little time to consider the matter. Meanwhile I will make inquiries; but, speaking off-hand, I should say that, owing to the present general depreciation of stock, it would be highly unadvisable for you to sell out, and my advice to you would be: Hold on to everything you've got.

"I am very glad you are pleased with your little house. We will let the matter of the rent stand over till your affairs are rather more in order than they are at present.—With kindest regards, very sincerely yours,

"HORATIO BYSSHE WADDINGTON.

"P.S.—I have settled with Palmer and Hoskins for the trellis and hot water rail."

"*To* Messrs. Lawson & Rutherford, Solicitors,

"9, Bedford Row, London, W.C.

"Dear Sirs,—Will you kindly advise me as to the current value of the following shares—namely:

"Fifty £5 5 per cent. New South American Rubber Syndicate;

"Fifty £10 10 per cent. B Preference Addison Railway, Nicaragua;

"One hundred £1 4 per cent. Welbeck Mutual Assurance Society.

"Would you recommend the holder to sell out at present prices? And should I be justified in accepting these shares as security for an immediate loan of five hundred?—Faithfully yours,

"HORATIO BYSSHE WADDINGTON."

He was expecting Elise for tea at four o'clock on Wednesday, and Messrs. Lawson and Rutherford's reply reached him very opportunely that afternoon.

"Dear Sir,—*Re* your inquiry in your letter of the twenty-fifth instant, as to the current value of 5 per cent. New South American Rubber Syndicate Shares, 10 per cent. B Preference Addison Railway, and 4 per cent. Welbeck Mutual Assurance Society, respectively, we beg to inform you that these stocks are seriously depreciated, and we doubt whether at the present moment the holder would find a purchaser. We certainly cannot advise you to accept them as security for the sum you name.—We are, faithfully,

"Lawson & Rutherford."

It was clear that poor Elise—who could never have had any head for business—was deceived as to the value of her securities. It might even be that with regard to all three of them she might have to cut her losses and estimate her income minus the dividends accruing from this source. But that only made it the more imperative that she should have at least a thousand pounds tucked snugly away in some safe investment. Nothing short of the addition of fifty pounds to her yearly income would enable Elise to pay her way. The dear woman's affairs ought to stand on a sound financial basis; and Mr. Waddington asked himself this question: Was he prepared to put them there? All that Elise could offer him, failing her depreciated securities, was the reversion of a legacy of five hundred pounds promised to her in her aunt's will. She had spoken very hopefully of this legacy. Was he prepared to fork out a whole five hundred pounds on the offchance of Elise's aunt dying within a reasonable time and making no alteration in her will? In a certain contingency he *was* prepared. He was prepared to do all that and more for Elise. But it was not possible, it was not decent to state his conditions to Elise beforehand, and in any case Mr. Waddington did not state them openly as conditions to himself. He allowed his mind to be muzzy on this point. He had no doubt whatever about his passion, but he preferred to contemplate the possibility of its satisfaction through a decent veil of muzziness. When he said to himself that he would like to know where he stood before committing himself, it was as near as he could get to clarity and candour.

And when he wrote to Elise that his promise was conditional he really did mean that the loan would depend on the value of the securities offered; a condition that his integrity could face, a condition that, as things stood, he had a perfect right to make. While, all the time, deep inside him was the knowledge that, if Elise gave herself to him, he would not ask for security— he would not make any conditions at all. He saw Elise, tender and yielding, in his arms; he saw himself, tender and powerful, stooping over her, and he thought, with a qualm of disgust: "I wouldn't touch her poor little legacy."

Meanwhile he judged it well to let the correspondence pass, like any other business correspondence, through his secretary's hands. It was well to let Barbara see that his relations with Mrs. Levitt were on a strictly business footing, that he had nothing to hide. It was well to have copies of the letters. It was well—Mr. Waddington's instinct, not his reason, told him it WA well—to have a trustworthy witness to all these transactions. A witness who understood the precise nature of his conditions, in the event, the highly unlikely event, of trouble with Elise later on. (It was almost as if, secretly, he had a premonition.) Also, when his conscience reproached him, as it did, with making conditions, with asking the dear woman for security, he was able to persuade himself that he didn't really mean it, that all this was clever camouflage designed to turn Barbara's suspicions, if she ever had any, off the scent. And at the same time he was not sorry that Barbara should see him in his rôle of generous benefactor and shrewd adviser.

"I needn't tell you, Barbara, that all this business is strictly private. As my confidential secretary, you have to know a great many things it wouldn't do to have talked about. You understand?"

"Perfectly."

She understood, too, that it was an end of the compact with Ralph Bevan. She must have foreseen this affair when she said to him there would be things she simply couldn't tell. Only she had supposed they would be things she would see, reward of clear eyesight, not things she would be regularly let in for knowing.

And her clear eyes saw through the camouflage. She had a suspicion.

"I don't see," she said, "why you should have to go without your rent just because Mrs. Levitt doesn't want to pay it."

She was sorry for Waddy. He might be ever so wise about Mrs. Levitt's affairs; but he was a perfect goose about his own. No wonder Fanny had asked her to take care of him.

"I've no doubt," he said, "she *wants* to pay it; but she's a war widow, Barbara, and she's hard up. I can't rush her for the rent."

"She's no business to rush you for trellis work and water pipes you didn't order."

"Well—well," he couldn't be angry with the child. She was so loyal, so careful of his interests. And he couldn't expect her to take kindly to Elise. There would be a natural jealousy. "That's Palmer and Hoskins's mistake. I can't haggle with a lady, Barbara. *Noblesse oblige.*" But he winced under her clear eyes.

She thought: "How about the fifty and the five hundred? At this rate *noblesse* might *oblige* him to do anything."

She could see through Mrs. Levitt.

Mr. Waddington kept on looking at the clock.

It was now ten minutes to four, and at any moment Elise might be there. His one idea was to get Barbara Madden out of the way. Those clear eyes were not the eyes he wanted to be looking at Elise, to be looking at him when *their* eyes met. And he understood that that fellow Bevan was going to call for her at four. He didn't want *him* about. "Where are you going for your walk?" he said.

"Oh, anywhere. Why?"

"Well, if you happen to be in Wyck, would you mind taking these photographs back to Pyecraft and showing him the ones I've chosen? Just see that he doesn't make any stupid mistake."

The photographs were staring her in the face on the writing-table, so that there was really no excuse for her forgetting them, as she did. But Mr. Waddington's experience was that if you wanted anything done you had to do it yourself.

2

Elise would be taken into the drawing-room. He went to wait for her there.

And as he walked up and down, restless, listening for the sound of her feet on the gravel drive and the ringing of the bell, at each turn of his steps he was arrested by his own portrait. It stared at him from its place above Fanny's writing-table; handsome, with its brilliant black and carmine, it gave him an uneasy sense of rivalry, as if he felt the disagreeable presence of a younger

- 94 -

man in the room. He stared back at it; he stared at himself in the great looking-glass over the chimneypiece beside it.

He remembered Fanny saying that she liked the iron-grey of his moustache and hair; it was more becoming than all that hard, shiny black. Fanny was right. It *was* more becoming. And his skin—the worn bloom of it, like a delicate sprinkling of powder. Better, more refined than that rich, high red of the younger man in the gilt frame. To be sure his eyes, blurred onyx, bulged out of creased pouches; but his nose—the Postlethwaite nose, a very handsome feature—lifted itself firmly above the fleshy sagging of the face. His lips pouted in pride. He could still console himself with the thought that mirrors were unfaithful; Elise would see him as he really was; not that discoloured and distorted image. He pushed out his great chest and drew a deep, robust breath. At the thought of Elise the pride, the rich, voluptuous, youthful pride of life mounted. And as he turned again he saw Fanny looking at him.

The twenty-year-old Fanny in her girl's white frock and blue sash; her tilted, Gainsborough face, mischievous and mocking, smiled as if she were making fun of him. His breath caught in his chest. Fanny—Fanny. His wife. Why hadn't his wife the loyalty and intelligence of Barbara, the enthusiasm, the seriousness of Elise? He needn't have any conscientious scruples on Fanny's account; she had driven him to Elise with her frivolity, her eternal smiling. Of course he knew that she cared for him, that he had power over her, that there had never been and never would be any other man for Fanny; but he couldn't go on with Fanny's levity for ever. He wanted something more; something sound and solid; something that Elise gave him and no other woman. Any man would want it.

And yet Fanny's image made him uneasy, watching him there, smiling, as if she knew all about Elise and smiled, pretending not to care. He didn't want Fanny to watch him with Elise. He didn't want Elise to see Fanny. When he looked at Fanny's portrait he felt again his old repugnance to their meeting. He didn't want Elise to sit in the same room with Fanny, to sit in Fanny's chair. The drawing-room was Fanny's room. The red dahlia and powder-blue parrot chintz was Fanny's choice; every table, cabinet and chair was in the place that Fanny had chosen for it. The book, the frivolous book she had been reading before she went away, lay on her little table. Fanny was Fanny and Elise was Elise.

He rang the bell and told Partridge to show Mrs. Levitt into the library and to bring tea there. The library was *his* room. He could do what he liked in it. The girl Fanny laughed at him out of the corners of her eyes as he went. Suddenly he felt tender and gentle to her, because of Elise.

When Elise came she found him seated in his armchair absorbed in a book. He rose in a dreamy attitude, as if he were still dazed and abstracted with his reading.

Thus, at the very start, he gave himself the advantage; he showed himself superior to Elise. Intellectually and morally superior.

"You're deep in it? I'm interrupting?" she said.

He came down from his height instantly. He was all hers.

"No. I was only trying to pass the time till you came."

"I'm late then?"

"Ten minutes." He smiled, indulgent

Elise was looking handsomer than ever. The light November chill had whipped a thin flush into her face. He watched her as she took off her dark skunk furs and her coat.

How delightful to watch a woman taking off her things, the pretty gestures of abandonment; the form emerging, slimmer. That was one of the things you thought and couldn't say. Supposing he had said it to Elise? Would she have minded?

"What are you thinking of?" she said.

"How did you know I was thinking of anything?"

"Your face. It tells tales."

"Only nice ones to you, my dear lady."

"Ah, but you *didn't* tell—"

"Would you like me to?"

"Not if it's naughty. Your face looks naughty."

He wheeled, delighted. "Now, how does my face look when it's naughty?"

"Oh, that *would* be telling. It's just as well you shouldn't know."

"Was it as naughty as all that then?"

"Yes. Or as nice."

They kept it up, lightly, till Partridge and Annie Trinder came, tinkling and rattling with the tea-things outside the door. As if, Mr. Waddington thought, they meant to warn them.

"Partridge," he called, as the butler was going, "Partridge, if Sir John Corbett calls you can show him in here; but I'm not at home to anybody else."

(Clever idea, that.)

"He isn't coming, is he, the tiresome old thing?"

"No. He isn't. If I thought he was for one minute I wouldn't be at home."

"Then why—?"

"Why did I say I would be? Because I wanted to make it safe for you, Elise."

Thus tactfully he let it dawn on her that he might be dangerous.

"We don't want to be interrupted, do we?" he said.

"Not by Sir John Corbett."

He drew up the big, padded sofa square before the fire for Elise. All his movements were unconscious, innocent of deliberation and design. He seated himself top-heavily behind the diminutive gate-legged tea-table; the teapot and cups were like dolls' things in his great hands. She looked at him, at his slow fingers fumbling with the sugar tongs.

"Would you like me to pour out tea for you?" she said.

He started visibly. He wouldn't like it at all. He wasn't going to allow Elise to put herself into Fanny's place, pouring out tea for him as if she was his wife. She wouldn't have suggested it if she had had any tact or any delicacy.

"No," he said. The "No" sounded hard and ungracious. "You must really let me have the pleasure of waiting on you."

The sugar dropped from the tongs; he fumbled again, madly, and Elise smiled. "Damn the tongs," he thought; "damn the sugar."

"Take it in your fingers, goose," she said.

Goose! An endearment, a caress. It softened him. His tenderness for Elise came back.

"My fingers are all thumbs," he said.

"Your thumbs, then. You don't suppose I mind?"

There was meaning in her voice, and Mr. Waddington conceived himself to be on the verge of the first exquisite intimacies of love. He left off thinking about Fanny. He poured out tea and handed bread and butter in a happy dream. He ate and drank without knowing what he ate and drank. His whole consciousness was one muzzy, heavy sense of the fullness and nearness of Elise. He could feel his ears go "vroom-vroom" and his voice thicken as if he were slightly, very slightly drunk. He wondered how Elise could go on eating bread and butter.

He heard himself sigh when at last he put her cup down.

He considered the position of the tea-table in relation to the sofa. It hemmed in that part of it where he was going to sit. Very cramping. He moved it well back and considered it again. It now stood in his direct line of retreat from the sofa to the armchair. An obstruction. If anybody were to come in. He moved it to one side.

"That's better," He said. "Now we can get a clear view of the fire. It isn't too much for you, Elise?"

He had persuaded himself that he had really moved the tea-table because of the fire. As yet he had no purpose and no plan. He didn't know what on earth he was going to say to Elise.

He sat down beside her and there was a sudden hushed pause. Elise had turned round in her seat and was looking at him; her eyes were steady behind the light tremor of their lashes, brilliant and profound. He reflected that her one weak point, the shortness of her legs, was not noticeable when she was sitting down. He also wondered how he could ever have thought her mouth hard. It moved with a little tender, sensitive twitch, like the flutter of her eyelids, and he conceived that she was drawn to him and held trembling by his fascination.

She spoke first.

"Mr. Waddington, I don't know how to thank you for your kindness about the rent. But you know it's safe, don't you?"

"Of course I know it. Don't talk about rent. Don't think about it."

"I can't help it. I can't think of anything else until it's paid."

"I'd rather you never paid any rent at all than that you should worry about it like this. I didn't ask you to come here to talk business, Elise."

"I'm afraid I must talk it. Just a little."

"Not now," he said firmly. "I won't listen."

It sounded exactly as if he said he wouldn't listen to any more talk about rent; but he thought: "I don't know what I shall do if she begins about that five hundred. But she hardly can, after that. Anyhow, I shall decline to discuss it."

"Tell me what you've been doing with yourself?"

"You can't *do* much with yourself in Wyck. I trot about my house—my dear little house that you've made so nice for me. I do my marketing, and I go out to tea with the parson's wife, or the doctor's wife, or Mrs. Bostock, or Mrs. Grainger."

"I didn't know you went to the Graingers."

He thought that was not very loyal of Elise.

"You must go somewhere."

"Well?"

"And in the evenings we play bridge."

"Who plays bridge?"

"Mr. Hawtrey, or Mr. Thurston, or young Hawtrey, and Toby, and Major Markham and me."

"Always Major Markham?"

"Well, he comes a good deal. He likes coming."

"*Does* he?"

"Do you mind?"

"I should mind very much if I thought it would make any difference."

"Any difference?" She frowned and blinked, as though she were trying hard to see what he meant, what he possibly *could* mean by that. "Difference?" she said. "To what?"

"To you and me."

"Of course it doesn't. Not a scrap. How could it?"

"No. How could it? I don't really believe it could."

"But why should it?" she persisted.

"Why, indeed. Ours is a wonderful relation. A unique relation. And I think you want as much as I do to—to keep it intact."

"Of course I want to keep it intact. I wouldn't for worlds let anything come between us, certainly not bridge." She meditated. "I suppose I do play rather a lot. There's nothing else to do, you see, and you get carried away."

"I hope, my dear, you don't play for money."

"Oh, well, it isn't much fun for the others if we don't."

"You don't play high, I hope?"

"What do you call high?"

"Well, breaking into pound notes."

"Pound notes! Penny points—well, ten shillings is the very highest stake when we're reckless and going it. Besides, I always play against Markham and Hawtrey, because I know *they* won't be hard on me if I lose."

"Now, *that's* what I don't like. I'd a thousand times rather pay your gambling debts than have you putting yourself under an obligation to those men."

He couldn't bear it. He couldn't bear to think that Elise could bear it.

"You should have come to me," he said.

"I have come to you, haven't I?" She thought of the five hundred pounds.

He thought of them too. "Ah, that's different. Now, about these debts to Markham and Hawtrey. How much do they come to—about?"

"Oh, a five-pound note would cover all of it. But I shall only be in debt to you."

"We'll say nothing about that. If I pay it, Elise, will you promise me you'll never play higher than penny points again?"

"It's too angelic of you, really."

He smiled. He liked paying her gambling debts. He liked the power it gave him over her. He liked to think that he could make her promise. He liked to be told he was angelic. It was all very cheap at five pounds, and it would enable him to refuse the five hundred with a better grace.

"Come, on your word of honour, only penny points."

"On my word of honour.... But, oh, I don't think I can take it."

She thought of the five hundred. When you wanted five hundred it was pretty rotten to be put off with a fiver.

"If you can take it from Hawtrey and Markham—"

"That's it. I *can't* take it from Markham. I haven't done that. I can't do it."

"Well, Hawtrey then."

"Hawtrey's different"

"Why is he different?"

A faint suspicion, relating to Markham, troubled him, and not for the first time.

"Well, you see, he's a middle-aged married man. He might be my uncle."

He thought: "And Markham—*he* might be—"

But Elise was not in love with the fellow. No, no. He was sure of Elise; he knew the symptoms; you couldn't mistake them. But she might marry Markham, all the same. Out of boredom, out of uncertainty, out of desperation. He was not going to let that happen; he would make it impossible; he would give Elise the certainty she wanted now.

"You said *I* was different."

Playful reproach. But she would understand.

"So you are. You're a married man, too, aren't you?"

"I thought we'd agreed to forget it."

"Forget it? Forget Mrs. Waddington?"

"Yes, forget her. You knew me long before you knew Fanny. What has she got to do with you and me?"

"Just this, that she's the only woman in the county who'll know *me*."

"Because you're my friend, Elise."

"You needn't remind me. I'm not likely to forget that any good thing that's come to me here has come through you."

"I don't want anything but good to come to you through me"

He leaned forward.

"You're not very happy in Wyck, are you?"

"Happy? Oh, yes. But it's not what you'd call wildly exciting. And Toby's worrying me. He says he can't stand it, and he wants to emigrate."

"Well, why not?"

Mr. Waddington's heart gave a great thump of hope. He saw it all clearly. Toby was the great obstruction. Elise might have held out for ever as long as Toby lived with her. But if Toby went—She saw it too; that was why she consented to his going.

"It isn't much of a job for him, Bostock's Bank."

"N-no," she assented, "n-no. I've told him he can go if he can get anything."

He played, stroking the long tails of her fur. It lay between them like a soft, supine animal.

"Would you like to live in Cheltenham, Elise?"

"Cheltenham?"

"If I took a little house for you?"

(He had calculated that he might just as well lose his rent in Cheltenham as in Wyck. Better. Besides, he needn't lose it. He could let the White House. It would partly pay for Cheltenham.)

"One of those little houses in Montpelier Place?"

"It's too sweet of you to think of it." She began playing too, stroking the fur animal; their hands played together over the sleek softness, consciously, shyly, without touching.

"But—why Cheltenham?"

"Cheltenham isn't Wyck."

"No. But it's just as dull and stuffy. Stuffier."

"Beautiful little town, Elise."

"What's the good of that when it's crammed full of school children and school teachers, and decayed army people and old maids? I don't *know* anybody in Cheltenham."

"Can't you see that that would be the advantage?"

"No. I can't see it. There's only one place I *want* to live in."

"And that is—?"

"London. And I can't."

"Why not?" After all, London was not such a bad idea. He had thought of it before now himself.

"Well—I don't know whether I told you that I'm not on very good terms with my husband's people. They haven't been at all nice to me since poor Frank's death."

"Poor Elise—"

"They live in London and they want to keep me out of it. My father-in-law gives me a small allowance on condition I don't live there. They hate me," she said, smiling, "as much as all that."

"Is it a large allowance?"

"No. It's a very small one. But they know I can't get on without it."

"You ought not to be dependent on such people.... Perhaps in a flat—or one of those little houses in St. John's Wood—"

"It would be too heavenly. But what's the good of talking about it?"

"You must know what I want to do for you, Elise. I want to make you happy, to put you safe above all these wretched worries, to take care of you, dear. You *will* let me, won't you?"

"My dear Mr. Waddington—my dear friend—" The dark eyes brightened. She saw a clear prospect of the five hundred. Compared with what old Waddy was proposing, such a sum, and a mere loan too, represented moderation. The moment had come, very happily, for reopening this question. "I can't let you do anything so—so extensive. Really and truly, all I want is just a temporary loan. If you really could lend me that five hundred. You said—"

"I didn't say I would. And I didn't say I wouldn't. I said it would depend."

"I know. But you never said on what. If the securities I offered you aren't good enough, there's the legacy."

He was silent. He knew now that his condition had had nothing to do with the securities. He must know, he would know, where he stood.

"My aunt," said Elise gently, "is very old."

"I wouldn't dream of touching your poor little legacy." He said it with passion. "Won't you drop all this sordid talk about business and trust me?"

"I do trust you."

The little white hand left off stroking the dark fur and reached out to him. He took it and held it tight. It struggled to withdraw itself.

"You aren't afraid of me?" he said.

"No, but I'm afraid of Partridge coming in and seeing us. He might think it rather odd."

"He won't come in. It doesn't matter what Partridge thinks."

"Oh, *doesn't* it!"

"He won't come in."

He drew a little closer to her.

"He will. He *will*. He'll come and clear away the things. I hear him coming."

He got up and went to the door of the smoke-room, to the further door, and looked out.

"There's no one there," he said. "They don't come 'till six and it isn't five yet.... Elise—abstract your mind one moment from Partridge. If I get that little house in London, will you live in it?"

"I can't let you. You make me ashamed, after all you've done for me. It's too much."

"It isn't. If I take it, will you let me come and see you?"

"Oh, yes. But—" She shrank, so far as Elise could be said to shrink, a little further back into her corner.

"It's rather far from Wyck," he said. "Still, I could run up once in"—he became pensive—"in three weeks or so."

"For the day—I should be delighted."

"No. *Not* for the day." He was irritated with this artificial obtuseness. "For the week-end. For the week, sometimes, when I can manage it. I shall say it's business."

She drew back and back, as if from his advance, her head tilted, her eyes glinting at him under lowered lids, taking it all in yet pretending a paralysis of ignorance. She wanted to see—to see how far he would go, before she—She wanted him to think she didn't understand him even now.

It was this half-fascinated, backward gesture that excited him. He drew himself close, close.

"Elise, it's no use pretending. You know what I mean. You know I want you."

He stooped over her, covering her with his great chest. He put his arms round her.

"In my arms. You *know* you want *me*—"

She felt his mouth pushed out to her mouth as it retreated, trying to cover it, to press down. She gave a cry: "Oh—oh, you—" and struggled, beating him off with one hand while the other fumbled madly for her pocket-handkerchief. His grip slackened. He rose to his feet. But he still stooped over her, penning her in with his outstretched arms, his weight propped by his hands laid on the back of the sofa.

"You—old—imbecile—" she spurted.

She could afford it. In one rapid flash of intelligence she had seen that, whatever happened, she could never get that five hundred pounds *down*. And to surrender to old Waddy without it, to surrender to old Waddy at all, when she could marry Freddy Markham, would be too preposterous. Even if there hadn't been any Freddy Markham, it would have been preposterous.

At that moment as she said it, while he still held her prisoned and they stared into each other's faces, she spurting and he panting, Barbara came in.

He started; jerked himself upright. Mrs. Levitt recovered herself.

"You silly cuckoo," she said. "You don't know how ridiculous you look."

She had found her pocket-handkerchief and was dabbing her eyes and mouth with it, rubbing off the uncleanness of his impact. "How ridic—Te-hee—Te-hee—te-hee!" She shook with laughter.

Barbara pretended not to see them. To have gone back at once, closing the door on them, would have been to admit that she had seen them. Instead she moved, quickly yet abstractedly, to the writing-table, took up the photographs and went out again.

Mr. Waddington had turned away and stood leaning against the chimneypiece, hiding his head ("Poor old ostrich!") in his hands. His attitude expressed a dignified sorrow and a wronged integrity. Barbara stood for a collected instant at the door and spoke:

"I'm sorry I forgot the photographs." As if she said: "Cheer up, old thing. I didn't really see you."

Through the closed door she heard Mrs. Levitt's laughter let loose, malignant, shrill, hysterical, a horrid sound.

"I'm sorry, Elise. But I thought you cared for me."

"You'd no business to think. And it wasn't likely I'd tell you."

"Oh, you didn't tell me, my dear. How could you? But you made me believe you wanted me."

"Wanted? Do you suppose I wanted to be made ridiculous?"

"Love isn't ridiculous," said Mr. Waddington.

"It is. It's *the* most ridiculous thing there is. And when *you're* making it.... If you could have seen your face—Oh, dear!"

"If you wouldn't laugh quite so loud. The servants will hear you."

"I mean them to hear me."

"Confound you, Elise!"

"That's right, swear at me. Swear at me."

"I'm sorry I swore. But, hang it all, it's every bit as bad for me as it is for you."

"Worse, I fancy. You needn't think Miss Madden didn't see you, because she did."

"It's a pity Miss Madden didn't come in a little sooner."

"Sooner? I think she chose her moment very well."

"If she had heard the whole of our conversation I think she'd have realized there was something to be said for me."

"There isn't anything to be said for you. And until you've apologized for insulting me—"

"You've heard me apologize. As for insulting you, no decent woman, in the circumstances, ever tells a man his love insults her, even if she can't return it."

"And even if he's another woman's husband?"

"Even if he's another woman's husband, if she's ever given him the right—"

"Right? Do you think you bought the right to make love to me?" She rose, confronting him.

"No. I thought you'd given it me…. I was mistaken."

He helped her to put on the coat that she wriggled into with clumsy, irritated movements. Clumsy. The woman *was* clumsy. He wondered how he had never seen it. And vulgar. Noisy and vulgar. You never knew what a woman was like till you'd seen her angry. He had answered her appropriately and with admirable tact. He had scored every point; he was scoring now with his cool, imperturbable politeness. He tried not to think about Barbara.

"Your fur."

"Thank you."

He rang the bell. Partridge appeared.

"Tell Kimber to bring the car round and drive Mrs. Levitt home."

"Thank you, Mr. Waddington, I'd rather walk."

Partridge retired.

She held out her hand. Mr. Waddington bowed abruptly, not taking it. He strode behind her to the door, through the smoke-room, to the further door. In the hall Partridge hovered. He left her to him.

And, as she followed Partridge across the wide lamp-lighted space, he noticed for the first time that Elise, in her agitation, waddled. Like a duck—a greedy duck. Like that horrible sister of hers, Bertha Rickards.

Then he thought of Barbara Madden.

3

When Ralph called for Barbara he told her, first thing, that he had heard from Mackintyres, the publishers, about his book. He had sent it them two-thirds finished, and Grevill Burton—"Grevill *Burton*, Barbara!"—had read it and reported very favourably. Mackintyres had agreed to publish it if the end was equal to the beginning and the middle.

It was this exciting news, thrown at her before she could get her hat on, that had caused Barbara to forget all about Mr. Waddington's photographs and Mr. Waddington's book and Mr. Waddington, until she and Ralph were half way between Wyck-on-the-Hill and Lower Speed. There was nothing for it then but to go on, taking care to get back in time to take the photographs to Pyecraft's before the shop closed. There hadn't been very much time, but Barbara said she could just do it if she made a dash, and it was the dash she made that precipitated her into the scene of Mr. Waddington's affair.

Ralph waited for her at the white gate.

"We must sprint," she said, "if we're to be in time."

They sprinted.

As they walked slowly back, Barbara became thoughtful.

As long as she lived she would remember Waddington: the stretched-out arms, the top-heavy body bowed to the caress; the inflamed and startled face staring at her, like some strange fish, over Mrs. Levitt's shoulder, the mouth dropping open as if it called out to her "Go back!" What depths of fatuity he must have sunk to before he could have come to that! And the sad figure leaning on the chimneypiece, whipped, beaten by Mrs. Levitt's laughter—the high, coarse, malignant laughter that had made her run to the smoke-room door to shield him, to shut it off.

What wouldn't Ralph have given to have seen him!

It was all very well for Ralph to talk about making a "study" of him; he hadn't got further than the merest outside fringe of his great subject. He didn't know the bare rudiments of Waddington. He had had brilliant flashes of his own, but no sure sight of the reality. And it had been given to her, Barbara, to see it, all at once. She had penetrated at one bound into the thick of him. They had wondered how far he would go; and he had gone so far, so incredibly far above and beyond himself that all their estimates were falsified.

And she saw that her seeing was the end—the end of their game, hers and Ralph's, the end of their compact, the end of the tie that bound them. She found herself shut in with Waddington; the secret that she shared with him shut Ralph out. It was intolerable that all this rich, exciting material should be left on her hands, lodged with her useless, when she thought of what she and Ralph could have made of it together.

If only she could have given it him. But of course she couldn't. She had always known there would be things she couldn't give him. She would go on seeing more and more of them.

Odd that she didn't feel any moral indignation. It had been too funny, like catching a child in some amusing naughtiness; and, as poor Waddy's eyes and open mouth had intimated, she had had no business to catch him, to know anything about it, no business to be there.

"Ralph," she said, "you must let me off the compact."

He turned, laughing. "Why, have you seen something?"

"It doesn't matter whether I have or haven't."

"It was a sacred compact."

"But if I can only keep it by being a perfect pig—"

He looked down at her face, her troubled, unnaturally earnest face.

"Of course, if you feel like that about it—"

"You'd feel like that if you were his confidential secretary and had all his correspondence."

"Yes, yes. I see, Barbara, it won't work. I'll let you off the compact. We can go on with him just the same."

"We can't."

"What? Not make a study of him?"

"No. We don't know what we're doing. It isn't safe. We may come on things any day."

"Like the thing you came on just now."

"I didn't say I'd come on anything."

"All right, you didn't. He shall be our unfinished book, Barbara."

"He'll be *your* unfinished book. I've finished mine all right. Anything else will be simply appendix."

"You think you've got him complete?"

"Fairly complete."

"Oh, Barbara—"

"Don't tempt me, Ralph."

"After all," he said, "we were only playing with him."

"Well, we mustn't do it again."

"Never any more?"

"Never any more. I know it's a game for gods; but it's a cruel game. We must give it up."

"You mean we must give him up?"

"Yes, we've hunted and hounded him enough. We must let him go."

"That's the compact, is it?"

"Yes."

"We shall break it, Barbara; see if we don't. We can't keep off him."

4

Mr. Waddington judged that, after all, owing to his consummate tact, he had scored in the disagreeable parting with Mrs. Levitt. But when he thought of Barbara, little Barbara, a flush mounted to his face, his ears, his forehead; he could feel it—wave after wave of hot, unpleasant shame.

He went slowly back to the library and shut himself in with the tea-table, and the sofa, and the cushions crushed, deeply hollowed with the large pressure of Elise. He wondered how much Barbara had taken in, at what precise moment she had appeared. He tried to reconstruct the scene. He had been leaning over Elise; he could see himself leaning over her, enclosing her, and Elise's head, stiffened, drawing back from his kiss. Worse than the sting of her repugnance was the thought that Barbara had seen it and his attitude, his really very compromising attitude. Had she? Had she? The door now, it was at right angles to the sofa; perhaps Barbara hadn't caught him fair. He went to the door and came in from it to make certain. Yes. Yes. From that point it was no good pretending that he couldn't be seen.

But Barbara had rushed in like a little whirlwind, and she had gone straight to the writing-table, turning her back. She wouldn't have had time to take it in. He was at the chimneypiece before she had turned again, before she could have seen him. He must have recovered himself when he heard her coming. She couldn't charge in like that without being heard. He must have been standing up, well apart from Elise, not leaning over her by the time Barbara came in.

He tried to remember what Barbara had said when she went out. She had said something. He couldn't remember what it was, but it had sounded reassuring. Now, surely if Barbara had seen anything she wouldn't have stopped at the door to say things. She would have gone straight out without a word. In fact, she wouldn't have come in at all. She would have drawn back the very instant that she saw. She would simply never have penetrated as far as the writing-table. He remembered how coolly she had taken up the photographs and gone out again as if nothing had happened.

Probably, then, as far as Barbara was concerned, nothing had happened.

Then he remembered the horrible laughing of Elise. Barbara must have heard that; she must have wondered. She might just have caught him with the tail of her eye, not enough to swear by, but enough to wonder; and afterwards she would have put that and that together.

And he would have to dine with her alone that evening, to face her young, clear, candid eyes.

He didn't know how he was going to get through with it, and yet he did get through.

To begin with, Barbara was very late for dinner.

She had thought of being late as a way of letting Mr. Waddington down easily. She would come in, smiling and apologetic, palpably in the wrong, having kept him waiting, and he would be gracious and forgive her, and his graciousnees and forgiveness would help to reinstate him. He would need, she reflected, a lot of reinstating. Barbara considered that, in the matter of punishment, he had had enough. Mrs. Levitt, with her "You old imbecile!" had done to him all, and more than all, that justice could require; there was a point of humiliation beyond which no human creature should be asked to suffer. To be caught making love to Mrs. Levitt and being called an old imbecile! And then to be pelted with indecent laughter. And, in any case, it was not her, Barbara's, place to punish him or judge him. She had had no business to catch him, no business, in the first instance, to forget the photographs.

Therefore, as she really wanted him not to know that she had caught him, she went on behaving as if nothing had happened. All through dinner she turned the conversation on to topics that would put him in a favourable or interesting light. She avoided the subject of Fanny. She asked him all sorts of questions about his war work.

"Tell me," she said, "some of the things you did when you were a special constable."

And he told her his great story. To be sure, she knew the best part of it already, because Ralph had told it—it had been one of his scores over her—but she wanted him to remember it. She judged that it was precisely the sort of memory that would reinstate him faster than anything. For really he had played a considerable part.

"Well"—you could see by his face that he was gratified—"one of the things we had to do was to drive about the villages and farms after dark to see that there weren't any lights showing. It was nineteen—yes—nineteen-sixteen, in the winter. Must have been winter, because I was wearing my British warm with the fur collar. And there was a regular scare on."

"Air raids?"

"No. Tramps. We'd been fairly terrorized by a nasty, dangerous sort of tramp. The police were looking for two of these fellows—discharged soldiers. We'd a warrant out for their arrest. Robbery and assault."

"With violence?"

"Well, you may call it violence. One of 'em had thrown a pint pot at the landlord of the King's Head and hurt him. And they'd bolted with two bottles of beer and a tin of Player's Navy Cut. They'd made off, goodness knows where. We couldn't find 'em.

"I was driving to Daunton on a very nasty, pitch-black night. You know how beastly dark it is between the woods at Byford Park? Well, I'd just got there when I passed two fellows skulking along under the wall. They stood back— it was rather a near shave with no proper lights on—and I flashed my electric torch full on them. Blest if they weren't the very chaps we were looking for. And I'd got to run 'em in somehow, all by myself. And two to one. It wasn't any joke, I can tell you. Goodness knows what nasty knives and things they might have had on 'em."

"What *did* you do?"

"Do? I drove on fifty yards ahead, and pulled up the car outside the porter's lodge at Byford. Then I got out and came on and met 'em. They were trying to bolt into the wood when I turned my torch on them again and shouted 'Halt!' in a parade voice.

"They halted, hands up to the salute. I thought the habit would be too much for 'em when they heard the word of command. I said, 'You've got to come along with me.' I didn't know how on earth I was going to take them if they wouldn't go. And they'd started dodging. So I tried it on again: 'Halt!' Regular parade stunt. And they halted again all right. Then I harangued them. I said, 'Shun, you blighters! I'm a special constable, and I've got a warrant here for your arrest.'

"I hadn't. I'd nothing but an Inland Revenue Income Tax form. But I whipped it out of my breast pocket and trained my light on the royal arms at the top. That was enough for 'em. Then I shouted again in my parade voice, 'Right about face! Quick march!'

"And I got them marching. I marched them the two miles from Byford, through Lower Speed, and up the hill to Wyck and into the police station. And we ran 'em in for robbery and assault."

"It was clever of you."

"No; nothing but presence of mind and bluff, and showing that you weren't going to stand any nonsense. But I don't suppose Corbett or Hawtrey or any of those chaps would have thought of it."

Barbara wondered: "Supposing I were to turn on him and say, 'You old humbug, you know I don't believe a word of it. You know you didn't march them a hundred yards.' Or '*I* saw you this afternoon.' What would he look like?" It was inconceivable that she should say these things. If she was to go on with her study of him alone she would go on in the spirit they had begun in, she and Ralph. That spirit admitted nothing but boundless amusement, boundless joy in him. Moral indignation would have been a false note; it would have been downright irreverence towards the God who made him.

What if he did omit to mention that the nasty, dangerous fellows turned out to be two feeble youths, half imbecile with shell-shock and half drunk, and that it was Mr. Hawtrey, arriving opportunely in his car, who took them over the last mile to the police station? As it happened Mr. Waddington had frankly forgotten these details as inessential to his story. (He *had* marched them a mile.)

After telling it he was so far re-established in his own esteem as to propose their working together on the Ramblings after dinner. He even ordered coffee to be served in the library, as if nothing had happened there. Unfortunately, by some culpable oversight of Annie Trinder's, the cushions still bore the imprint of Elise. Awful realization came to him when Barbara, with a glance at the sofa, declined to sit on it. He had turned just in time to catch the flick of what in a bantering mood he had once called her "Barbaric smile." After all, she might have seen something. Not Mrs. Levitt's laughter but the thought of what Barbara might have seen was his punishment—that and being alone with her, knowing that she knew.

5

All this happened on a Wednesday, and Fanny wouldn't be back before Saturday. He had three whole days to be alone with Barbara.

He had thought that no punishment could be worse than that, but as the three days passed and Barbara continued to behave as though nothing had happened, he got used to it. It was on a Friday night, as he lay awake, reviewing for the hundredth time the situation, that his conscience pointed out to him how he really stood. There was a worse punishment than Barbara's knowing.

If Fanny knew—

There were all sorts of ways in which she might get to know. Barbara might tell her. The two were as thick as thieves. And if the child turned jealous and hysterical—She had never liked Elise. Or she might tell Ralph Bevan and he might tell Fanny, or he might tell somebody who would tell her. There were always plenty of people about who considered it their duty to report these things.

Of course, if he threw himself on Barbara's mercy, and exacted a promise from her not to tell, he knew she would keep it. But supposing all the time she hadn't seen or suspected anything? Supposing her calm manner came from a mind innocent of all seeing and suspecting? Then he would have given himself away for nothing.

Besides, even if Barbara never said anything, there was Elise. No knowing what Elise might do or say in her vulgar fury. She might tell Toby or Markham, and the two might make themselves damnably unpleasant.
The story would be all over the county in no time.

And there were the servants. Supposing one of the women took it into her head to give notice on account of "goings on?"

He couldn't live in peace so long as all or any of these things were possible.

The only thing was to be beforehand with Barbara and Bevan and Elise and Toby and Markham and the servants; to tell Fanny himself before any of them could get in first. The more he thought about it the more he was persuaded that this was the only right, the only straightforward and manly thing to do; at the same time it occurred to him that by suppressing a few unimportant details he could really give a very satisfactory account of the whole affair. It would not be necessary, for instance, to tell Fanny what his intentions had been, if indeed he had ever had any. For, as he went again and again over the whole stupid business, his intentions—those that related to the little house in Cheltenham or St. John's Wood—tended to sink back into the dream state from which they had arisen, clearing his conscience more and more from any actual offence. He had, in fact, nothing to account for but his attitude, the rather compromising attitude in which Barbara had found him. And that could be very easily explained away. Fanny was not one of those exacting, jealous women; she would be ready to accept a reasonable explanation of anything. And you could always appease her by a little attention.

So on Friday afternoon Mr. Waddington himself drove the car down to Wyck Station and met Fanny on the platform. He made tea for her himself and waited on her, moving assiduously, and smiling an affectionate yet rather conscious smile. He was impelled to these acts spontaneously, because of that gentleness and tenderness towards Fanny which the bare thought of Elise was always enough to inspire him with.

Thus, by sticking close to Fanny all the evening he contrived that Barbara should have no opportunity of saying anything to her. And in the last hour before bed-time, when they were alone together in the drawing-room, he began.

He closed the door carefully behind Barbara and came back to his place, scowling like one overpowered by anxious thought. He exaggerated this expression on purpose, so that Fanny should notice it and give him his opening, which she did.

"Well, old thing, what are *you* looking so glum about?"

"Do I look glum?"

"Dismal. What is it?"

He stood upright before the chinmeypiece, his conscience sustained by this posture of rectitude.

"I'm not quite easy about Barbara," he said.

"Barbara? What on earth has *she* been doing?"

"She's been doing nothing. It's—it's rather what she may do if you don't stop her."

"I don't want to stop her," said Fanny, "if you're thinking of Ralph Bevan."

"Ralph Bevan? I certainly am not thinking of him. Neither is she."

"Well then, what?"

"I was thinking of myself."

"My dear, you surely don't imagine that Barbara's thinking of you?"

"Not—not in the way you imply. The fact is, I was let in for a—a rather unpleasant scene the other day with Mrs. Levitt."

"I always thought," said Fanny, "that woman would let you in for something. Well?"

"Well, I hardly know how to tell you about it, my dear."

"Why, was it as bad as all that? Perhaps I'd better not know."

"I want you to know. I'm trying to tell you—because of Barbara."

"I can't see where Barbara comes in."

"She came into the library while it was happening—"

Fanny laughed and it disconcerted him.

"While what was happening?" she said. "You'd better tell me straight out. I don't suppose it was anything like as bad as you think it was."

"I'm only afraid of what Barbara might think."

"Oh, you can trust Barbara not to think things. She never does."

Dear Fanny. He would have found his job of explaining atrociously difficult with any other woman. Any other woman would have entangled him tighter and tighter; but he could see that Fanny was trying to get it straight, to help him out with all his honour and self-respect and dignity intact. Every turn she gave to the conversation favoured him.

"My dear, I'm afraid she saw something that I must say was open to misinterpretation. It wasn't my fault, but—"

No. The better he remembered it the more clearly he saw it was Elise's fault, not his. And he could see that Fanny thought it was Elise's fault. This suggested the next step in the course that was only not perjury because it was so purely instinctive, the subterfuge of terrified vanity. It seemed to him that he had no plan; that he followed Fanny.

"Upon my word I'd tell you straight out, Fanny, only I don't like to give the poor woman away."

"Mrs. Levitt?" said Fanny. "You needn't mind. You may be quite sure that she'll give *you* away if you don't."

She was giving him a clear lead.

When he began he had really had some thoughts of owning, somewhere about this point, that he had lost his head; but when it came to the point he saw that this admission was unnecessarily quixotic, and that he would be far safer if he suggested that Elise had lost hers. In fact, it was Fanny who had suggested it in the first place. It might not be altogether a fair imputation, but, hang it all, it was the only one that would really appease Fanny, and he had Fanny to think of and not Elise. He owed it her. For her sake he must give up the personal luxury of truthtelling. The thing would go no further with Fanny, and it was only what Fanny had believed herself in any case and always would believe. Elise would be no worse off as far as Fanny was concerned. So he fairly let himself go.

"There's no knowing what she may do," he said. "She was in a thoroughly hysterical state. She'd come to me with her usual troubles—not able to pay her rent, and so on—and in talking she became very much upset and er— er—lost her head and took me completely by surprise."

"That," he thought, "she certainly did."

"You mean you lost yours too?" said Fanny mildly.

"I did nothing of the sort. But I was rather alarmed. Before you could say 'knife' she'd gone off into a violent fit of hysterics, and I was just trying to bring her round when Barbara came in." His explanation was so much more plausible than the reality that he almost believed it himself. "I think," he said, pensively, "she *must* have seen me bending over her."

"And she didn't offer to help?"

"No; she rushed in and she rushed out again. She may not have seen anything; but in case she did, I wish, my dear, you'd explain."

"I think I'd better not," said Fanny, "in case she didn't."

"No. But it worries me every time I think of it. She came right into the room. Besides," he said, "we've got to think of Mrs. Levitt."

"Mrs. Levitt?"

"Yes. Put yourself in her place. She wouldn't like it supposed that I was making love to her. She might consider the whole thing made her look as ridiculous as it made me."

"I'd forgotten Mrs. Levitt's point of view. You rather gave me to understand that was what she wanted."

"I never said anything of the sort." Seeing that the explanation was going so well he could afford to be magnanimous.

"I must have imagined it," said Fanny. "She recovered, I suppose, and you got rid of her?"

"Yes, I got rid of her all right."

"Well," said Fanny, gathering herself up to go to bed, "I shouldn't worry any more about it. I'll make it straight with Barbara."

She went up to Barbara's bedroom, where Barbara, still dressed, sat reading over the fire.

"Come in, you darling," Barbara said. She got up and crouched on the hearthrug, leaving her chair for Fanny.

Fanny came in and sat down.

"Barbara," she said, "what's all this about Horatio and Mrs. Levitt?"

"I don't know," said Barbara flatly, with sudden presence of mind.

"I said you didn't. But the poor old thing goes on and on about it. He thinks you saw something the other day. Something you didn't understand. Did you?"

Barbara said nothing. She stared away from Fanny.

"Did you?"

"Of course I didn't."

"Of course you did. He says you must have seen. And it's worrying him no end."

"I saw something. But he needn't worry. I understood all right"

"What did you see?"

"Nothing. Nothing that mattered."

"It matters most awfully to me."

"I don't think it need," said Barbara.

"But it *does*. In a sense I don't mind what he does, and in a sense I do. I still care enough for that."

"I don't think there was anything you need mind so awfully."

"Yes, but there *was* something. He said there was. He was afraid you'd misunderstand it. He said he was bending over her when you came in."

"Well, he *was* bending a bit."

"What was *she* doing?"

"She was laughing."

"In hysterics?"

She saw it all.

"I suppose you might call it hysterics. They weren't nice hysterics, though. She isn't a nice woman."

"No. But he was making love to her, and she was laughing at him. She was nice enough for that."

"If that's nice."

"Why, what else could the poor woman do if she's honest?"

"Oh, she's honest enough in *that* way," said Barbara.

"And he couldn't see it. He's so intent on his own beautiful Postlethwaite nose, he can't see anything that goes on under it.... Still, honest or not honest, she's a beast, Barbara. When they'd been such pals and he'd helped her, to have gone and rounded on the poor thing like that. She might just as well have pulled his Postlethwaite nose. It couldn't have hurt more."

"Oh, I think he'll get over it."

"I mean it couldn't have hurt *me* more."

"She *is* a beast," said Barbara. "I bet you anything you like it's her fault. She drove him to it."

"No, Barbara, it was *my* fault. *I* drove him. I'm always laughing at him, and he can't bear being laughed at. It makes him feel all stuffy and middle-aged. He only goes in for passion because it makes him feel young."

"It isn't really passion," said Barbara.

"No, you wise thing, it isn't. If it was I could forgive him. I could forgive it if he really felt young. It's this ghastly affectation I can't stand.... But it's my fault, Barbara, my fault. I should have kept him young...."

They sat silent, Barbara at Fanny's feet. Presently Fanny drew the girl's head down into her lap.

"You'll never be old, Barbara," she said. "And Ralph won't."

"What made you think of Ralph, Fanny?"

"Horatio, of course."

XII

1

If any rumour circulated round Wyck-on-the-Hill, sooner or later it was bound to reach the old lady at the Dower House. The Dower House was the redistributing centre for the news of the district.

Thus Mr. Waddington heard that Mrs. Levitt was talking about letting the White House furnished; that she was in debt to all the tradesmen in the place; that her rent at Mrs. Trinder's was still owing; that her losses at bridge were never paid for. He heard that if Major Markham had been thinking of Mrs. Levitt, he had changed his mind; there was even a definite rumour about a broken engagement. Anyhow, Major Markham was now paying unmistakable attentions to the youngest Miss Hawtrey of Medlicott. But as, engagement or no engagement, his attentions to Mrs. Levitt had been unmistakable too, their rupture required some explanation. It was supposed that the letter which the Major's mother, old Mrs. Markham of Medlicott, received from her daughter, Mrs. Dick Benham of Tunbridge Wells, did very thoroughly explain it. There had been "things" in that letter which Mrs. Markham had not been able to repeat, but you gathered from her singular reticence that they had something to do with Dick Benham and Mrs. Levitt, and that they showed conclusively that Elise was not what old Mrs. Waddington called "a nice woman."

"They say she led Frank Levitt an awful life. The Benhams, my dear, won't have her in the house."

But all this was trivial compared with the correspondence that now passed between Mr. Waddington and Elise. He admitted now that old Corbett had known what he was talking about when he had warned him that he would be landed—landed, if he didn't take care, to the tune of five hundred and fifty-five pounds. His letters to Mrs. Levitt, dictated to Barbara Madden, revealed the care he had to take. From motives which appeared to him chivalrous he had refrained from showing Barbara Mrs. Levitt's letters to him. He left her to gather their crude substance from his admirable replies.

"'MY DEAR MRS. LEVITT:

"'I am afraid I must advise you to give up the scheme if it depends on my co-operation. I thought I had defined my position—'

"Defined my position is good, I think."

"It sounds good," said Barbara.

"'That position remains what it was. And as your exceptionally fine intelligence cannot fail to understand it, no more need be said.

"'At least I hope it is so. I should be sorry if our very pleasant relations terminated in disappointment—'"

For one instant she could see him smile, feeling voluptuously the sharp, bright edge of his word before it cut him. He drew back, scowling above a sudden sombre flush of memory.

"Disappointment—" said Barbara, giving him his cue.

"Disappointment is not quite the word. I want something—something more chivalrous."

His eyes turned away from her, pretending to look for it.

"Ah—now I have it. 'Very pleasant relations terminated on a note—on a note of—on an unexpected note.

"'With kind regards, very sincerely yours,

"'HORATIO BYSSHE WADDINGTON.'

"You will see, Barbara, that I am saying precisely the same thing, but saying it inoffensively, as a gentleman should."

Forty-eight hours later he dictated:

"'DEAR MRS. LEVITT:

"'No: I have no suggestion to make except that you curtail your very considerable expenditure. For the rest, believe me it is as disagreeable for me to be obliged to refuse your request as I am sure it must be for you to make it—'

"H'm. Rest—request. That won't do. 'As disagreeable for me to have to refuse as it must be for you to ask.'

"Simpler, that. Never use an elaborate phrase where a simple one will do.

"'You are good enough to say I have done so much for you in the past. I have done what I could; but you will pardon me if I say there is a limit beyond which I cannot go.

"'Sincerely yours,

"'HORATIO B. WADDINGTON.'

"I've sent her a cheque for fifty-five pounds already. That ought to have settled her."

"Settled her? You don't mean to say you sent her a *cheque?*"

"I did."

"You oughtn't to have sent her anything at all."

"But I'd promised it, Barbara—"

"I don't care. You ought to have waited."

"I wanted to close the account and have done with her."

"That isn't the way to close it, sending cheques. That cheque will have to go through Parson's Bank. Supposing Toby sees it?"

"What if he does?"

"He might object. He might even make a row about it."

"What could I do? I had to pay her."

"You could have made the cheque payable to me. It would have passed as my quarter's salary. I could have cashed it and you could have given her notes."

"And if Toby remembered their numbers?"

"You could have changed them for ten shilling notes in Cheltenham."

"All these elaborate precautions!"

"You can't be too precautions when you're dealing with a woman like that.... Is this all you've given her?"

"All?"

"Yes. Did you ever give her anything any other time?"

"Well—possibly—from time to time—"

"Have you any idea of the total amount?"

"I can't say off-hand. And I can't see what it has to do with it."

"It has everything to do with it. Can you find out?"

"Certainly, if I look up my old cheque books."

"You'd better do that now."

He turned, gloomily, to his writing-table. The cheque books for the current year and the year before it betrayed various small loans to Mrs. Levitt, amounting in all to a hundred and fifty pounds odd.

"Oh, dear," said Barbara, "all that's down against you. Still—it's all ante-Wednesday. What a pity you didn't pay her that fifty-five before your interview."

"How do you mean?"

"It's pretty certain she's misinterpreted your paying it now so soon."

"After the interview? Do you really think she misunderstood me, Barbara?"

"I think she wants you to think she did."

"You think she's trying—trying—to—"

"To sell you her silence? Yes, I do."

"Good God! I never thought of that. Blackmail."

"I don't suppose for a minute she thinks she's blackmailing you. She's just trying it on.... And she may raise her price, too. She won't rest till she's got that five hundred out of you."

Mrs. Levitt's next communication would appear to have supported Barbara's suspicion, for Mr. Waddington was compelled to answer it thus:

"DEAR MRS. LEVITT:

"You say you were 'right then' and that my 'promises' were 'conditional'"—

(You could tell where the inverted commas came by the biting clip of his tone.)

—"I fail to appreciate the point of this allusion. I cannot imagine what conditions you refer to. I made none. As for promises, I am not responsible for the somewhat restricted interpretation you see fit to put on a friend's general expressions of goodwill.

"Yours truly,

"HORATIO BYSSHE WADDINGTON."

His last letter, a day later, never got as far as its signature.

"DEAR MADAM:

"My decision will not be affected by the contingency you suggest. You are at perfect liberty to say what you like. Nobody will believe you."

"That, I think, is as far as I can go."

"Much too far," said Barbara.

"And that's taking her too seriously."

"Much. You mustn't send that letter."

"Why not?"

"Because it gives you away."

"Gives me away? It seems to me most guarded."

"It isn't. It implies that there *are* things she might say. Even if you don't mind her saying them you mustn't put it in writing."

"Ah-h. There's something in that. Of course, I could threaten her with a lawyer's letter. But somehow—The fact is, Barbara, if you're a decent man you're handicapped in dealing with a lady. Delicacy. There are things that could be said. Material things—most material to the case. But I can't say them."

"No. You can't say them. But I can. I think I could stop the whole thing in five minutes, if I saw Mrs. Levitt. Will you leave it to me?"

"Come—I don't know—"

"Why not? I assure you it'll be all right."

"Well. Perhaps. It's a matter of business. A pure matter of business."

"It certainly is that. There's no reason why you shouldn't hand it over to your secretary."

He hesitated. He was still afraid of what Elise might say to Barbara.

"You will understand that she is in a very unbalanced state. Excitable. A woman in that state is apt to put interpretations on the most innocent—er—acts."

"She won't be able to put on any after I've done with her. If it comes to that, I can put on interpretations too."

Mr. Waddington then, at Barbara's dictation, wrote a short note to Mrs. Levitt inviting her to call and see him that afternoon at three o'clock.

2

At three o'clock Barbara was ready for her.

She had assumed for the occasion her War Office manner, that firm sweetness with which she used to stand between importunate interviewers and her chief. It had made her the joy of her department.

"Mr. Waddington is extremely sorry he is not able to see you himself. He is engaged with his agent at the moment."

Mr. Waddington had, indeed, created that engagement.

"Engaged? But I have an appointment."

"Yes. He's very sorry. He said if there was anything I could do for you—"

"Thank you, Miss Madden. If it's all the same to you, I'd much rather see Mr. Waddington himself. I can wait."

"I wouldn't advise you to. I'm afraid he may be a long time. He has some very important business on hand just now."

"*My* business," said Mrs. Levitt, "is very important."

"Oh, if it's only business," Barbara said, "I think we can settle it at once. I've had most of the correspondence in my hands and I think I know all the circumstances."

"You have had the correspondence in your hands?"

"Well, you see, I'm Mr. Waddington's secretary. That's what I'm here for."

"I didn't know he trusted his private business to his secretary."

"He's obliged to. He has so much of it. You surely don't expect him to copy out his own letters?"

"I don't expect him to hand over my letters to other people to read."

"I haven't read your letters, Mrs. Levitt. I've merely taken down his answers to copy out and file for reference."

"Then, my dear Miss Madden, you don't know all the circumstances."

"At any rate, I can tell you what Mr. Waddington intends to do and what he doesn't. You want to see him, I suppose, about the loan for the investment?"

Mrs. Levitt was too profoundly disconcerted to reply.

Barbara went on in her firm sweetness. "I know he's very sorry not to be able to do more, but, as you know, he did not advise the investment and he can't possibly advance anything for it beyond the fifty pounds he has already paid you."

"Since you know so much about it," said Mrs. Levitt with a certain calm, subdued truculence, "you may as well know everything. You are quite mistaken in supposing that Mr. Waddington did not advise the investment. On the contrary, it was on his representations that I decided to invest. And it was on the strength of the security he offered that my solicitors advanced me the money. He is responsible for the whole business; he has made me enter into engagements that I cannot meet without him, and when I ask him to fulfil his pledges he lets me down."

"I don't think Mr. Waddington knows that your solicitors advanced the money. There is no reference to them in the correspondence."

"I think, if you'll look through your *files*, or if Mr. Waddington will look through his, you'll find you are mistaken."

"I can tell Mr. Waddington what you've told me and let you know what he says. If you don't mind waiting a minute I can let you know now."

She sought out Mr. Waddington in his office—luckily it was situated in the kitchen wing, the one farthest from the library. She found him alone in it (the agent had gone), sitting in a hard Windsor chair. He knew that Elise couldn't pursue him into his office; it was even doubtful whether she knew where it was. He had retreated into it as into some impregnable position.

Not that he looked safe. His face sagged more than ever, as though the Postlethwaite nose had withdrawn its support from that pale flesh of funk. If it had any clear meaning at all it expressed a terrified expectation of blackmail. His very moustache and hair drooped lamentably.

"Are you disengaged?" she said.

"Yes. But for God's sake don't tell her that."

"It's all right. She knows she isn't going to see you."

"Well?"

She felt the queer, pathetic clinging of his mind to her as if it realized that she held his honour and Fanny's happiness in her hands.

"She's not going to give up that five hundred without a struggle."

"The deuce she isn't. On what grounds does she claim it?"

"She says you advised her to make a certain investment, and that you promised to lend her half the sum she wanted."

"I made no promise. I said, 'Perhaps that sum might be forthcoming.' I made it very clear that it would depend on circumstances."

"On circumstances that she understood—knew about?"

"Er—on circumstances that—No. She didn't know about them."

"Still, you made conditions?"

"No. I made—a mental reservation."

"She seems to be aware of the circumstances that influenced you. She thinks you've gone back on your word."

"I have gone back on nothing. My word's sacred. The woman lies."

"She sticks to it that the promise was made, that on the strength of it she invested a certain sum of money through her solicitors, that they advanced the money on that security and you advised the investment."

"I did not advise it. I advised her to give it up. I wrote to her. You took down the letter.... No, you didn't. I copied that one myself."

"Have you got it? I'd better show it her."

"Yes. It's—it's—confound it, it's in my private drawer."

"Can't I find it?"

He hesitated. He didn't like the idea of anybody, even little Barbara, rummaging in his private drawer, but he had to choose the lesser of two evils, and that letter would put the matter beyond a doubt.

"Here's the key," he said, and gave it her. "It's dated October the thirtieth or thirty-first. But it's all humbug. I've reason to believe that money was never invested at all. It's all debts. She hasn't a leg to stand on. Not a leg."

"Not a stump," said Barbara. "Leave her to me."

She went back to the library. Mrs. Levitt's face lifted itself in excited questioning.

"One moment, Mrs. Levitt."

After a slightly prolonged search in Mr. Waddington's private drawer she found the letter of October tie thirty-first, and returned with it to the office. It was very short and clear:

"MY DEAR ELISE:

"I cannot promise anything—it depends on circumstances. But if you sent me the name and address of your solicitors it might help."

"Take it," he said, "and show it her."

3

Barbara went back again to the library and her final battle with Elise.

This time she had armed herself with the cheque books.

Mrs. Levitt began, "Well—?"

"Mr. Waddington says he is very sorry if there's any misunderstanding. I don't know whether you remember getting this letter from him?"

Mrs. Levitt blinked hard as she read the letter.

"Of course I remember."

"You see that he could hardly have stated his position more clearly."

"But—this letter is dated October the thirty-first. The promise I refer to was made long after that."

"It doesn't appear so from his letters—all that I've taken down. If you can show me anything in writing—"

"Writing? Mr. Waddington is a gentleman and he was my friend. I never dreamed of pinning him down to promises in writing. I thought his word was enough. I never dreamed of his going back on it. And after compromising me the way he's done."

Barbara's eyebrows lifted delicately, innocently. "*Has* he compromised you?"

"He has."

"How?"

"Never mind how. Quite enough to start all sorts of unpleasant stories."

"You shouldn't listen to them. People will tell stories without anything to start them."

"That doesn't make them any less unpleasant. I should have thought the very least Mr. Waddington could do—"

"Would be to pay you compensation?"

"There can be no compensation in a case of this sort, Miss Madden. I'm not talking about compensation. Mr. Waddington must realize that he cannot compromise me without compromising himself."

"I should think he would realize it, you know."

"Then he ought to realize that he is not exactly in a position to repudiate his engagements."

"Do you consider that *you* are in a position—exactly—to hold him to engagements he never entered into?"

"I've told you already that he has let me in for engagements that I cannot meet if he goes back on his word."

"I see. And you want to make it unpleasant for him. As unpleasant as you possibly can?"

"I can make it even more unpleasant for him, Miss Madden, than it is for me."

"What, after all the compromising?"

"I think so. If, for instance, I chose to tell somebody what happened the other day, what you saw yourself."

"*Did* I see anything?"

"You can't deny that you saw something you were not meant to see."

"You mean Wednesday afternoon? Well, if Mr. Waddington chose to say that I saw you in a bad fit of hysterics I shouldn't deny *that*."

"I see. You're well posted, Miss Madden."

"I am, rather. But supposing you told everybody in the place he was caught making love to you, what good would it do you?"

"Excuse me, we're not talking about the good it would do me, but the harm it would do him."

"Same thing," said Barbara. "Supposing you told everybody and nobody believed you?"

"Everybody will believe me. You forget that those stories have been going about long before Wednesday."

"All the better for Mr. Waddington and all the worse for you. You were compromised before Wednesday. Then why, if you didn't like being compromised, did you consent to come to tea alone with him when his wife was away?"

"I came on business, *as you know*."

"You came to borrow money from a man who had compromised you? If you're so careful of your reputation I should have thought that would have been the last thing you'd have done."

"You're forgetting my friendship with Mr. Waddington."

"You said business just now. Friendship or business, or business *and* friendship, I don't think you're making out a very good case for yourself, Mrs. Levitt. But supposing you did make it out, and supposing Mr. Waddington did lose his head and *was* making love to you on Wednesday, do you imagine people here are going to take *your* part against *him*?"

"He's not so popular in Wyck as all that."

"He mayn't be, but his caste is. Immensely popular with the county, which I suppose is all you care about. You must remember, Mrs. Levitt, that he's Mr. Waddington of Wyck; you're not fighting one Mr. Waddington, but three hundred years of Waddingtons. You're up against all his ancestors."

"I don't care *that* for his ancestors," said Mrs. Levitt with a gesture of the thumb.

"You may not. I certainly don't. But other people do. Major Markham, the Hawtreys, the Thurstons, even the Corbetts, do you suppose they're all going to turn against him because he lost his head for a minute on a Wednesday? Ten to one they'll all think, and *say*, you made him do it."

"I made him? Preposterous!"

"Not so preposterous as you imagine. You must make allowances for people's prejudices. If you wanted to stand clear you shouldn't have taken all that money from him."

"All that money indeed! A loan, a mere temporary loan, for an investment he recommended."

"Not only that loan, but—" Barbara produced the cheque books with their damning counterfoils. "Look here—twenty-five pounds on the thirty-first of January. And here—October last year, and July, and January before that— More than a hundred and fifty altogether. How are you going to account for that?

"And who's going to believe that Mr. Waddington paid all that for nothing, if some particularly nasty person gets up and says he didn't? You see what a horrible position you'd be in, don't you?"

Mrs. Levitt didn't answer. Her face thickened slightly with a dreadful flush. Her nerve was going.

Barbara watched it go. She followed up her advantage. "And supposing I were to tell everybody—his friend, Major Markham, say—that you were pressing him for that five hundred, immediately *after* the affair of Wednesday, on threats of exposure, wouldn't that look very like blackmail?"

"Blackmail? *Really*, Miss Madden—"

"I don't suppose you *mean* it for blackmail; I'm only pointing out what it'll look like. It won't look *well*.... Much better face the facts. You *can't* do Mr. Waddington any real harm, short of forcing his wife to get a separation."

There was a black gleam in Mrs. Levitt's eyes. "Precisely. And supposing— since we *are* supposing—I told Mrs. Waddington of his behaviour?"

"Too late. Mr. Waddington has told her himself."

"His own version."

"Certainly, his own version."

"And supposing I gave mine?"

"Do. Whatever you say it'll be your word against ours and she won't believe you. If she did she'd think it was all your fault.... And remember, I have the evidence for your attempts at blackmail.

"I don't think," said Barbara, going to the door and opening it, "there's anything more to be said."

Mrs. Levitt walked out with her agitated waddle. Barbara followed her amicably to the front door. There Elise made her last stand.

"*Good* afternoon, Miss Madden. I congratulate Mr. Waddington—on the partnership."

Barbara rushed to the relief of the besieged in his office redoubt.

"It's all over!" she shouted at him joyously.

Mr. Waddington did not answer all at once. He was still sitting in his uneasy Windsor chair, absorbed in meditation. He had brought out a little note from his inmost pocket and as he looked at it he smiled.

It began thus, and its date was the Saturday following that dreadful Wednesday:

"MY DEAR MR. WADDINGTON:

"After the way you have stood by me and helped me in the past, I cannot believe that it is all over, and that I can come to you, my generous friend, and be repulsed—"

He looked up. "How did she behave, Barbara?" "Oh—she wanted to bite— to bite badly; but I drew all her teeth, very gently, one by one." Teeth. Elise's teeth—drawn by Barbara.

He tore the note into little bits, and, as he watched them flutter into the waste-paper basket, he sighed. He rose heavily.

"Let's go and tell Fanny all about it," said Barbara.

XIII

1

"I hope you realize, Horatio, that it was Barbara who got you out of that mess?"

"Barbara showed a great deal of intelligence; but you must give me credit for some tact and discretion of my own," Mr. Waddington said as he left the drawing-room.

"*Was* he tactful and discreet?"

"His first letters," said Barbara, "were masterpieces of tact and discretion. Before he saw the danger. Afterwards I think his nerve may have gone a bit. Whose wouldn't?"

"It *was* clever of you, Barbara. All the same, it must have been rather awful, going for her like that."

"Yes."

Now that it was all over Barbara saw that it had been awful; rather like a dog-fight. She had been going round and round, rolling with Mrs. Levitt in the mud; so much mud that for purposes of sheer cleanliness it hardly seemed to matter which of them was top dog at the finish. All she could see was that it had to be done and there wasn't anybody else to do it.

"You see," Fanny went on, "she had a sort of case. He *was* making love to her and she didn't like it. It doesn't seem quite fair to turn on her after that."

"She did all the turning. I wouldn't have said a thing if she hadn't tried to put the screw on. Somebody had got to stop it."

"Yes," Fanny said. "Yes. Still, I wish we could have let her go in peace."

"There wasn't any peace for her to go in; and she wouldn't have gone. She'd have been here now, with his poor thumb in her screw. After all, Fanny, I only pointed out how beastly it would be for her if she didn't go. And I only did that because he was your husband, and it was your thumb, really."

"Yes, darling, yes; I know what you did it for. ... Oh, I wish she wasn't so horribly badly off."

"So do I, then it wouldn't have happened. But how can you be such an angel to her, Fanny?"

"I'm not. I'm only decent. I hate using our position to break her poor back. Telling her we're Waddingtons of Wyck and she's only Mrs. Levitt."

"It was the handiest weapon. And you didn't use it. *I'm* not a Waddington of Wyck. Besides, it's true; she can't blackmail him in his own county. You don't seem to realize how horrid she was, and how jolly dangerous."

"No," Fanny said, "I don't realize people's horridness. As for danger, I don't want to disparage your performance, Barbara, but she seems to me to have been an easy prey."

"You *are* disparaging me," said Barbara.

"I'm not. I only don't like to think of you enjoying that nasty scrap."

"I only enjoyed it on your account."

"And I oughtn't to grudge you your enjoyment when we reap the benefit. I don't know what Horatio would have done without you. I shudder to think of the mess he'd have made of it himself."

"He was making rather a mess of it," Barbara said, "when I took it on."

"Well," said Fanny, "I daresay I'm a goose. Perhaps I ought to be grateful to Mrs. Levitt. If he was on the look-out for adventures, it's just as well he hit on one that'll keep him off it for the future. She'd have been far more deadly if she'd been a nice woman. If he *must* make love."

"Only then he couldn't very well have done it," Barbara said.

"Oh, couldn't he! You never can tell what a man'll do, once he's begun," said Fanny.

2

Meanwhile Mrs. Levitt stayed on, having failed to let her house for the winter. She seemed to be acting on Barbara's advice and refraining from any malignant activity; for no report of the Waddington affair had as yet penetrated into the tea-parties and little dinners at Wyck-on-the-Hill. Punctually every Friday evening Mr. Thurston of the Elms, and either Mr. Hawtrey or young Hawtrey of Medlicott, turned up at the White House for their bridge. If Mrs. Dick Benham chose to write venomous letters about Elise Levitt to old Mrs. Markham, that was no reason why they should throw over an agreeable woman whose hospitality had made Wyck-on-the-Hill a place to live in, so long as she behaved decently *in* the place. They kept it up till past midnight now that Mrs. Levitt had had the happy idea of serving a delicious supper at eleven. (She had paid her debts of honour with Mr. Waddington's five pounds; the fifty she reserved, in fancy, for the cost of the chickens and the trifles and the Sauterne.) In Mr. Thurston and the Hawtreys the bridge habit and the supper habit, and what Billy Hawtrey called the Levitty habit, was so strong that it overrode their sense of loyalty to Major Markham. The impression created by Mrs. Dick Benham only heightened their enjoyment in doing every Friday what Mrs. Thurston and Mrs. Hawtrey persisted in regarding as a risky thing. "There was no harm in Elise Levitt," they said.

So every Friday, after midnight, respectable householders, sleeping on either side of the White House, were wakened by the sudden opening of her door, by shrill "Good nights" called out from the threshold and answered by bass voices up the street, by the shutting of the door and the shriek of the bolt as it slid to.

And the Rector went about saying, in his genial way, that he liked Mrs. Levitt, that she was well connected, and that there was no harm in her. So long as any parishioner was a frequent attendant at church, and a regular subscriber to the coal and blanket club, and a reliable source of soup and puddings for the poor, it was hard to persuade him that there was any harm in them. Fanny Waddington said of him that if Beelzebub subscribed to his coal and blanket club he'd ask him to tea. He had a stiff face for uncharitable people; Elise was received almost ostentatiously at the rectory as a protest against scandalmongering; and he made a point of stopping to talk to her when he met her in the street.

This might have meant the complete rehabilitation of Elise, but that the Rector's geniality was too indiscriminate, too perfunctory, too Christian, as Fanny put it, to afford any sound social protection; and, ultimately, the approval of the rectory was disastrous to Elise, letting her in, as she afterwards complained bitterly, for Miss Gregg. Meanwhile it helped her with people like Mrs. Bostock and Mrs. Cleaver and Mrs. Jackson, who wanted to be charitable and to stand well with the Rector.

Then, in the December following the Waddington affair, Wyck was astonished by the friendship that sprang up, suddenly, between Mrs. Levitt and Miss Gregg, the governess at the rectory.

There was a reason for it—there always is a reason for these things—and Mrs. Bostock named it when she named young Billy Hawtrey. Friendship with Mrs. Levitt provided Miss Gregg with, unlimited facilities for meeting Billy, who was always running over from Medlicott to the White House. Miss Gregg's passion for young Billy hung by so slender, so nervous, and so insecure a thread that it required the continual support of conversation with an experienced and sympathetic friend. Miss Gregg had never known anybody so sympathetic and so experienced as Mrs. Levitt. The first time they were alone together she had seen by Elise's face that she had some secret like her own (Miss Gregg meant Major Markham), and that she would understand. And one strict confidence leading to another, before very long Miss Gregg had captured that part of Elise's secret that related to Mr. Waddington.

It was through Miss Gregg's subsequent activities that it first became known in Wyck that Mrs. Levitt had referred to Mr. Waddington as "that horrible old man." This might have been very damaging to Mr. Waddington but that Annie Trinder, at the Manor, had told her aunt, Mrs. Trinder, that Mr. Waddington spoke of Mrs. Levitt as "that horrible woman," and had given orders that she was not to be admitted if she called. It was then felt that there might possibly be more than one side to the question.

Then, bit by bit, through the repeated indiscretions of Miss Gregg, the whole affair of Mrs. Levitt and Mr. Waddington came out. It travelled direct from Miss Gregg to the younger Miss Hawtrey of Medlicott, and finally reached Sir John Corbett by way of old Hawtrey, who had it from his wife, who didn't believe a word of it.

Sir John didn't believe a word of it, either. At any rate, that was what he said to Lady Corbett. To himself he wondered whether there wasn't "something in it." He would give a good deal to know, and he made up his mind that the next time he saw Waddington he'd get it out of him.

He saw him the very next day.

Ever since that dreadful Wednesday an uneasy mind had kept Mr. Waddington for ever calling on his neighbours. He wanted to find out from their behaviour and their faces whether they knew anything and how much they knew. He lived in perpetual fear of what that horrible woman might say or do. The memory of what *he* had said and done that Wednesday no longer disturbed his complete satisfaction with himself. He couldn't think of Elise as horrible without at the same time thinking of himself as the pure and chivalrous spirit that had resisted her. Automatically he thought of himself as pure and chivalrous. And in the rare but beastly moments when he did remember what he had done and said to Elise and what Elise had done and said to him, when he felt again her hand beating him off and heard her voice crying out: "You old imbecile!" automatically he thought of her as cold. Some women were like that—cold. Deficient in natural feeling. Only an abnormal coldness could have made her repulse him as she did. She had told him to his face, in her indecent way, that love was *the* most ridiculous thing. He couldn't, for the life of him, understand how a thing that was so delightful to other women could be ridiculous to Elise; but there it was.

Absolutely abnormal, that. His vanity received immense consolation in thinking of Elise as abnormal.

His mind passed without a jolt or a jar from one consideration to its opposite. Elise was cold and he was normally and nobly passionate Elise was horrible and he was chivalrously pure. Whichever way he had it he was consoled.

But you couldn't tell in what awful light the thing might present itself to other people.

It was this doubt that drove him to Underwoods one afternoon early in January, ostensibly to deliver his greetings for the New Year.

After tea Sir John lured him into his library for a smoke. The peculiar smile and twinkle at play on his fat face should have warned Mr. Waddington of what was imminent.

They puffed in an amicable silence for about two minutes before he began.

"Ever see anything of Mrs. Levitt now?"

Mr. Waddington raised his eyebrows as if surprised at this impertinence. He seemed to be debating with himself whether he would condescend to answer it or not.

"No," he said presently, "I don't."

"Taken my advice and dropped it, have you?"

"I should say, rather, it dropped itself."

"I'm glad to hear that, Waddington; I'm very glad to hear it. I always said, you know, you'd get landed if you didn't look out."

"My dear Corbett, I did look out. You don't imagine I was going to be let in more than I could help."

"Wise after the event, what?"

Mr. Waddington thought: "He's trying to pump me." He was determined not to be pumped. Corbett should not get anything out of him.

"After what event? Fanny's called several times, but she doesn't care to keep it up. Neither, to tell the honest truth, do I.... Why?"

Sir John was twinkling at him in his exasperating way.

"Why? Because, my dear fellow, the woman's going about everywhere saying she's given *you* up."

"I don't care," said Mr. Waddington, "what she says. Quite immaterial to me."

"You mayn't care, but your friends do, Waddington."

"It's very good of them. But they can save themselves the trouble."

He thought: "He isn't going to get anything out of me."

"Oh, come, you don't suppose we believe a word of it."

They looked at each other. Sir John thought: "I'll get it out of him." And Mr. Waddington thought: "I'll get it out of him."

"You might as well tell me what you're talking about," he said.

"My dear chap, it's what Mrs. Levitt's talking about. That's the point."

"Mrs. Levitt!"

"Yes. She's a dangerous woman, Waddington. I told you you were doing a risky thing taking up with her like that.... And there's Hawtrey doing the same thing, the very same thing.... But he's a middle-aged man, so I suppose he thinks he's safe. ... But if he was ten years younger— Hang it all, Waddington, if I was a younger man I shouldn't feel safe. I shouldn't, really. I can't think what there is about her. There's something."

"Yes," said Mr. Waddington, "there's something."

Something. He wasn't going to let Corbett think him so middle-aged that he was impervious to its charm.

"What is it?" said Sir John. "She isn't handsome, yet she gets all the young fellows running after her. There was Markham, and Thurston, and there's young Hawtrey. It's only sober old chaps like me who don't get landed.... Upon my word, Waddington, I shouldn't blame you if you *had* lost your head."

Mr. Waddington felt shaken in his determination not to let Corbett get it out of him. It was also clear that, if he did admit to having for one wild moment lost his head, Corbett would think none the worse of him. He would then be classed with Markham and young Billy, whereas if he denied it, he would only rank himself with old fossils like Corbett. And he couldn't bear it. There was such a thing as doing yourself an unnecessary injustice.

Sir John watched him hovering round the trap he had laid for him.

"Absolutely between ourselves," he said. "*Did* you?"

Under Mr. Waddington's iron-grey moustache you could see the Rabelaisian smile answering the Rabelaisian twinkle. For the life of him he couldn't resist it.

"Well—between ourselves, Corbett, absolutely—to be perfectly honest, I did. There *is* something about her.... Just for a second, you know. It didn't come to anything."

"Didn't it? She says you made violent love to her."

"I won't swear what I wouldn't have done if I hadn't pulled myself up in time."

At this point it occurred to him that if Elise had betrayed the secret of his love-making she would also have told her own tale of its repulse. That had to be accounted for.

"I can tell you one queer thing about that woman, Corbett. She's cold—cold."

"Oh, come, Waddington—"

"You wouldn't think it—"

"I don't," said Sir John, with a loud guffaw.

"But I assure you, my dear Corbett, she's simply wooden. Talk of making love, you might as well make love to—to a chair or a cabinet. I can tell you Markham's had a lucky escape."

"I don't imagine that's what put him off," said Sir John. "He knew something."

"What do you suppose he knew?"

"Something the Benhams told them, I fancy. They'd some queer story. Rather think she ran after Dicky, and Mrs. Benham didn't like it."

"Don't know what she wanted with him. Couldn't have been in love with him, I will say that for her."

"Well, she seems to have preferred their bungalow to her own. Anyhow, they couldn't get her out of it."

"I don't believe that story. We must be fair to the woman, Corbett."

He thought he had really done it very well. Not only had he accounted honourably for his repulse, but he had cleared Elise. And he had cleared himself from the ghastly imputation of middle-age. Repulse or no repulse, he was proud of his spurt of youthful passion.

And in another minute he had persuaded himself that his main motive had been the desire to be fair to Elise.

"H'm! I don't know about being fair," said Sir John. "Anyhow, I congratulate you on your lucky escape."

Mr. Waddington rose to go. "Of course—about what I told you—you won't let it go any further?"

Sir John laughed out loud. "Of course I won't. Only wanted to know how far *you* went. Might have gone farther and fared worse, what?"

He rose, too, laughing. "If anybody tries to pump me I shall say you behaved very well. So you did, my dear fellow, so you did. Considering the provocation."

He could afford to laugh. He had got it out of poor old Waddington, as he said he would. But to the eternal honour of Sir John Corbett, it did not go any further. When people tried to get it out of him he simply said that there was nothing in it, and that to his certain knowledge Waddington had behaved very well. As Barbara had prophesied, nobody believed that he had behaved otherwise. It was not for nothing that he was Mr. Waddington of Wyck.

And in consequence of the revelations she had made to her friend, Miss Gregg, very early in the New Year Elise found other doors closed to her besides the Markhams' and the Waddingtons'. And behind the doors on each side of the White House respectable householders could sleep in their beds on Friday nights without fear of being wakened by the opening and shutting of Mrs. Levitt's door and by the shrill "Good nights" called out from its threshold and answered up the street The merry bridge parties and the little suppers were no more.

Even the Rector's geniality grew more and more Christian and perfunctory, till he too left off stopping to talk to Mrs. Levitt when he met her in the street.

3

Mr. Waddington's confession to Sir John was about the only statement relating to the Waddington affair which did not go any further. Thus a very curious and interesting report of it reached Ralph Bevan through Colonel Grainger, when he heard for the first time of the part Barbara had played in it.

In the story Elise had told in strict confidence to Miss Gregg, Mr. Waddington had been deadly afraid of her and had beaten a cowardly retreat behind Barbara's big guns. Not that either Elise or Miss Gregg would have admitted for one moment that her guns were big; Colonel Grainger had merely inferred the deadliness of her fire from the demoralization of the enemy.

"Your little lady, Bevan," he said, "seems to have come off best in that encounter."

"We needn't worry any more about the compact, Barbara, now I know about it," Ralph said, as they walked together. Snow had fallen. The Cotswolds were all white, netted with the purplish brown filigree-work of the trees. Their feet went crunching through the furry crystals of the snow.

"No. That's one good thing she's done."

"Was it very funny, your scrap?"

"It seemed funnier at the time than it did afterwards. It was really rather beastly. Fanny didn't like it."

"You could hardly expect her to. There's a limit to Fanny's sense of humour."

"There's a limit to mine. Fanny was right. I had to fight her with the filthiest weapons. I had to tell her she couldn't do anything because he was Waddington of Wyck, and she was up against all his ancestors. I had to drag in his ancestors."

"That was bad."

"I know it was. It's what Fanny hated. And no wonder. She made me feel such a miserable little snob, Ralph."

"Fanny did?"

"Yes. *She* couldn't have done it. She'd have let her do her damnedest."

"That's because Fanny's an incurable little aristocrat. She's got more Waddington of Wyckedness in her little finger than Horatio has in all his ego; and she despises Mrs. Levitt. She wouldn't have condescended to scrap with her."

"The horrible thing is, it's true. He can do what he likes and nothing happens to him. He can turn the Ballingers out of their house and nothing happens. He can make love to a woman who doesn't want to be made love to and nothing happens. Because he's Waddington of Wyck."

"He's Waddington of Wyck, but he isn't such a bad old thing, really. People laugh at him, but they like him because he's so funny. And they've taken Mrs. Levitt's measure pretty accurately."

"You don't think, then, I was too big a beast to her?"

Ralph laughed.

"Somebody had to save him, Ralph. After all, he's Fanny's husband."

"Yes, after all, he's Fanny's husband."

"So you don't—do you?"

"Of course I don't.... What's he doing now?"

"Oh, just pottering about with his book. It's nearly finished."

"You've kept it up?"

"Rather. There isn't a sentence he mightn't have written himself. I think I'm going to let him go back to Lower Wyck on the last page and end there. In his Manor. I thought of putting something in about holly-decked halls and

Yule logs on the Christmas hearth. He was photographed the other day. In the snow."

"Gorgeous."

"I wonder if he'll really settle down now. Or if he'll do it all over again some day with somebody else."

"You can't tell. You can't possibly tell. He may do anything."

"That's what we feel about him," Barbara said.

"Endless possibilities. Yet you'd think he couldn't go one better than Mrs. Levitt."

For the next half-mile they disputed whether in the scene with Mrs. Levitt he was or was not really funny. Ralph was inclined to think that he might have been purely disgusting.

"You didn't *see* him, Ralph. You've no right to say he wasn't funny."

"No. No. I didn't see him. You needn't rub it in, Barbara."

"We've got to wait and see what he does next. It may be your turn any day."

"We can't expect him to do very much for a little while. He must be a bit exhausted with this last stunt."

"Yes. And the funny thing is he has moments when you don't laugh at him. Moments of calm, beautiful peace.... You come on him walking in his garden looking for snowdrops in the snow. Or he's sitting in his library, reading Buchan's 'History of the Great War.' Happy. Not thinking about himself at all. Then you're sorry you ever laughed at him."

"I'm not," Ralph said. "He owes it us. He does nothing else to justify his existence."

"Yes. But he exists. He exists. And somehow, it's pretty mysterious when you think of it. You wonder whether you mayn't have seen him all wrong. Whether all the time he isn't just, a simple old thing. When you get that feeling—of his mysteriousness, Ralph—somehow you're done."

"I haven't had it yet."

"Oh, it's there. You'll get it some day."

"You see, Barbara, how right I was? We can't keep off him."

XIV

1

It was Sunday, the last week of Horry's holidays. All through supper he had been talking about cycling to Cirencester if the frost held, to skate on the canal.

The frost did hold, and in the morning he strapped a cushion on the carrier of his bicycle and called up the stairs to Barbara.

"Come along, Barbara, let's go to Cirencester."

Barbara appeared, ready, carrying her skates. Mr. Waddington had let her off the Ramblings, yet, all of a sudden, she looked depressed.

"Oh, Horry," she said, "I was going with Ralph."

"You are *not*," said Horry. "You're always going with Ralph. You're jolly well coming with me this time."

"But I promised him."

"You'd no business to promise him, when it's the last week of my holidays. 'Tisn't fair."

Fanny came out into the hall.

"Horry," she said, "don't worry Barbara. Can't you see she wants to go with Ralph?"

"That's exactly," he said, "what I complain of."

She shook her head at him. "You're your father all over again," she said.

"I'll swear I'm not," said Horry.

"If you were half as polite as your father it wouldn't be a bad thing."

There was a sound of explosions in the drive. "There's Ralph come to settle it himself," said Fanny. And at that point, Mr. Waddington came out on them, suddenly, from the cloak-room.

"What's all this?" he said. He looked with disgust at the skates dangling from Barbara's hand. He went out into the porch and looked with disgust at Ralph and at the motor-bicycles. He thought with bitterness of the Cirencester canal. He couldn't skate. Even when he was Horry's age he hadn't skated. He couldn't ride a motor-bicycle. When he looked at the beastly things and thought of their complicated machinery and their evil fascination for Barbara, he hated them. He hated Horry and Ralph standing up before Barbara, handsome, vibrating with youth and health and energy.

"I won't have Barbara riding on that thing. It isn't safe. If he skids on the snow he'll break her neck."

"Much more likely to break his own neck," said Horry.

In his savage interior Mr. Waddington wished he would, and Horry too.

"He won't skid," said Barbara; "if he does I'll hop off."

"We'll come back," said Ralph, "if we don't get on all right."

They started in a duet of explosions, the motor-bicycles hissing and crunching through the light snow. Barbara, swinging on Ralph's carrier, waved her hand light-heartedly to Mr. Waddington. He hated Barbara; but far more than Barbara he hated Horry, and far more than Horry he hated Ralph.

"He'd no business to take her," he said. "She'd no business to go."

"You can't stop them, my dear," said Fanny; "they're too young."

"Well, if they come back with their necks broken they'll have only themselves to thank."

He took a ferocious pleasure in thinking of Horry and Ralph and Barbara with their necks broken.

Fanny stared at him. "I wonder what's made him so cross," she thought. "He looks as if he'd got a chill on the liver.".... "Horatio, have you got a chill on the liver?"

"Now, what on earth put that into your head?"

"Your face. You look just a little off colour, darling."

At that moment Mr. Waddington began to sneeze.

"There, I knew you'd caught cold. You oughtn't to go standing about in draughts."

"I haven't caught cold," said Mr. Waddington.

But he shut himself up in his library and stayed there, huddled in his armchair. From time to time he leaned forward and stooped over the hearth, holding his chest and stomach as near as possible to the fire. Shivers like thin icicles kept on slipping down his spine.

At lunch-time he complained that there was nothing he could eat, and before the meal was over he went back to his library and his fire. Fanny sat with him there.

"I wish you wouldn't go standing out in the cold," she said. She knew that on Saturday he had stood for more than ten minutes in the fallen snow of the park to be photographed. And he wouldn't wear his overcoat because he thought he looked younger without it, and slenderer.

"No wonder you've got a chill," she said.

"I didn't get it then. I got it yesterday in the garden."

She remembered. He had been wandering about the garden, after church, looking for snowdrops in the snow. Barbara had worn the snowdrops in the breast of her gown last night.

He nourished his resentment on that memory and on the thought that he had got his chill picking snowdrops for Barbara.

At tea-time he drank a little tea, but he couldn't eat anything. He felt sick and his head ached. At dinner-time, on Fanny's advice, he went to bed and Fanny took his temperature.

A hundred and one. He turned the thermometer in his hand, gazing earnestly at the slender silver thread. He was gratified to know that his temperature was a hundred and one and that Fanny was frightened and had sent for the doctor. He had a queer, satisfied, exalted feeling, now that he was in for it. When Barbara came back she would know what he was in for and be frightened, too. He would have been still more gratified if he had known that without him dinner was a miserable affair. Fanny showed that she was frightened, and her fear flattened down the high spirits of Ralph and Barbara and Horry, returned from their skating.

"You see, Barbara," said Ralph, when they had left Fanny and Horry with the doctor, "we can't live without him."

They listened at the smoke-room door for the sound of Dr. Ransome's departure, and Ralph waited while Barbara went back and brought him the verdict.

"It's flu, and a touch of congestion of the lungs."

They looked at each other sorrowfully, so sorrowfully that they smiled.

"Yet we can smile," he said.

"You know," said Barbara, "he got it standing in the snow, while Pyecraft photographed him."

"It's the way," Ralph said, "he would get it."

And Barbara laughed. But, all the same, she felt a distinct pang at her heart every time she went into her bedroom and saw, in its glass on her dressing-table, the bunch of snowdrops that Mr. Waddington had picked for her in the snow. They made a pattern on her mind; white cones hanging down; sharp green blades piercing; green stalks held in the crystal of the water.

2

"Nobody but a fool," said Horry, "would have stood out in the snow to be photographed … at his age."

"Don't, Horry."

Barbara was in the morning-room, stirring some black, sticky stuff in a saucepan over the fire. The black, sticky stuff was to go on Mr. Waddington's chest. Horry looked on, standing beside her in an attitude of impatience. A pair of boots with skates clipped on hung from his shoulders by their laces. He felt that his irritation was justifiable, for Barbara had refused to go out skating with him.

"Why 'don't'?" said Horry. "It's obvious."

"Very. But he's ill."

"There can't be much the matter with him or the mater wouldn't look so chirpy."

"She likes nursing him."

"Well," Horry said, "*you* can't nurse him."

"No. But I can stir this stuff," said Barbara.

"I suppose," Horry said, "you'd think me an awful brute if I went?"

"I wish you *would* go. You're a much more awful brute standing there saying things about him and getting in my way."

"All right. I'll get out of it. That's jolly easy."

And he went. But he felt sick and sore. He had tried to persuade himself that his father wasn't ill because he couldn't bear to think how ill he was; it interfered with his enjoyment of his skating. "If," he said to himself, "if he'd only put it off till the ice gave. But it was just like him to choose a hard frost."

His anger gave him relief from the sickening anxiety he felt when he thought of his father and his father's temperature. It had gone down, but not to normal.

Mr. Waddington lay in his bed in Fanny's room. Barbara, standing at the open door with her saucepan, caught a sight of him.

He was propped up by his pillows. On his shoulders, over one of those striped pyjama suits that Barbara had once ordered from the Stores, he wore, like a shawl, a woolly, fawn-coloured motor-scarf of Fanny's. His arms were laid before him on the counterpane in a gesture of complete surrender to his illness. Fanny was always tucking them away under the blankets, but if anybody came in he would have them so. He was sitting up, waiting in an adorable patience for something to be done for him. His face had the calm, happy look of expectation utterly appeased and resigned. It was that look that frightened Barbara; it made her think that Mr. Waddington was going to die. Supposing his congestion turned to pneumonia? There was so much of him to be ill, and those big men always did die when they got pneumonia.

Mr. Waddington could hear Barbara's quiet voice saying something to Fanny; he could see her unhappy, anxious face. He enjoyed Barbara's anxiety. He enjoyed the cause of it, his illness. So long as he was actually alive he even enjoyed the thought that, if his congestion turned to pneumonia, he might actually die. There was a dignity, a prestige about being dead that appealed to him. Even his high temperature and his headache and his shooting pains and his difficulty in breathing could not altogether spoil his pleasure in the delicious concern of everybody about him, and in his exquisite certainty that, at any minute, a moan would bring Fanny to his side. He was the one person in the house that counted. He had always known it, but he had never felt it with the same intensity as now. The mind of every person in the house was concentrated on him now as it had not been concentrated before. He was holding them all in a tension of worry and anxiety. He would apologize very sweetly for the trouble he was giving everybody, declaring that it made him very uncomfortable; but even Fanny could see that he was gratified.

And as he got worse—before he became too ill to think about it at all—he had a muzzy yet pleasurable sense that everybody in Wyck-on-the-Hill and in the county for miles round was thinking of him. He knew that Corbett and Lady Corbett and Markham and Thurston and the Hawtreys, and the Rector and the Rector's wife and Colonel Grainger had called repeatedly to inquire for him. He was particularly gratified by Grainger's calling. He knew that Hitchin had stopped Horry in the street to ask after him, and he was particularly gratified by that. Old Susan-Nanna had come up from Medlicott to see him. And Ralph Bevan called every day. That gratified him, too.

The only person who was not allowed to know anything about his illness was his mother, for Mr. Waddington was certain it would kill her. Every evening at medicine time he would ask the same questions: "My mother doesn't know yet?" And: "Anybody called to-day?" And Fanny would give him the messages, and he would receive them with a gentle, solemn sweetness. You wouldn't have believed, Barbara said to herself, that complacency could take so heartrending a form.

And under it all, a deeper bliss in bliss, was the thought that Barbara was thinking about him, worrying about him, and being, probably, ten times more unhappy about him than Fanny. After working so long by his side, her separation from him would be intolerable to Barbara; intolerable, very likely, the thought that it was Fanny's turn, now, to be by his side. Every day she brought him a bunch of snowdrops, and every day, as the door closed on her little anxious face, he was sorry for Barbara shut out from his room. Poor little Barbara. Sometimes, when he was feeling well enough, he would call to her: "Come in, Barbara." And she would come in and look at him and put her flowers into his hand and say she hoped he was better. And he would answer: "Not much better, Barbara. I'm very ill."

He even allowed Ralph to come and look at him. He would hold his hand in a clasp that he made as limp as possible, on purpose, and would say in a voice artificially weakened: "I'm very ill, Ralph."

Dr. Ransome said he wasn't; but Mr. Waddington knew better. It was true that from time to time he rallied sufficiently to comb his own hair before Barbara was let in with her snowdrops, and that he could give orders to Partridge in a loud, firm tone; but he was too ill to do more than whisper huskily to Barbara and Fanny.

Then when he felt a little better the trained nurse came, and with the sheer excitement of her coming Mr. Waddington's temperature leapt up again, and the doctor owned that he didn't like that.

And Barbara found Fanny in the library, crying. She had been tidying up his writing-table, going over all his papers with a feather brush, and she had come on the manuscript of the Ramblings unfinished.

"Fanny—"

"Barbara, I know I'm an idiot, but I simply cannot bear it. It was all very well as long as I could nurse him, but now that woman's come there's nothing I can do for him.... I've—I've never done anything all my life for him. He's always done everything for me. And I've been a brute. Always laughing at him.... Think, Barbara, think; for eighteen years never to have taken him seriously. Never since I married him.... I believe he's going to die. Just—just to punish me."

"He isn't," said Barbara indignantly, as if she had never believed it herself. "The doctor says he isn't really very ill. The congestion isn't spreading. It was better yesterday."

"It'll be worse to-night, you may depend on it. The doctor doesn't *like* his temperature flying up and down like that."

"It'll go down again," said Barbara.

"You don't know what it'll do," said Fanny darkly. "Did you ever see such a lamb, such a *lamb* as he is when he's ill?"

"No," said Barbara; "he's an angel."

"That's just," said Fanny, "what makes me feel he's going to die…. I wish I were you, Barbara."

"Me?"

"Yes. You've really helped him. He could never have written his book without you. His poor book."

She sat stroking it. And suddenly a horrible memory overcame her, and she cried out:

"Oh, my God! And I've laughed at that, too!"

Barbara put her arm round her. "You didn't, darling. Well, if you did—it is a little funny, you know. I'm afraid I've laughed a bit."

"Oh, *you*—that doesn't matter. You helped to write it."

Then Barbara broke out. "Oh, don't, Fanny, don't, *don't* talk about his poor book. I can't *bear* it."

"We're both idiots," said Fanny. "Imbeciles."

She paused, drying her eyes.

"He liked the snowdrops you brought him," she said.

Barbara thought: "And the snowdrops he brought *me*." He had caught cold that day, picking them. They had withered in the glass in her bedroom.

She left Fanny, only to come upon Horry in his agony. Horry stood in the window of the dining-room, staring out and scowling at the snow.

"Damn the snow!" he said. "It's killed him."

"It hasn't, Horry," she said; "he'll get better."

"He won't get better. If this beastly frost holds he hasn't got a chance."

"Horry dear, the doctor says he's better."

"He doesn't. He says his temperature's got no business to go up."

"All the same—"

"Supposing he does think him better. Supposing he doesn't know. Supposing he's a bleating idiot…. I expect the dear old pater knows how he is a jolly sight better than anybody can tell him…. And you know you're worrying about him yourself. So's the mater. She's been crying."

"She's jealous of the nurse. That's what's the matter with her."

"Jealous? Tosh! That nurse is an idiot. She's sent his temperature up first thing."

"Horry, old thing, you must buck up. You mustn't let your nerve go like this."

"Nerve? Your nerve would go if you were me. I tell you, Barbara, I wouldn't care a hang about his being ill—I mean I shouldn't care so infernally if I'd been decent to him. ... But you were right I was a cad, a swine. Laughing at him."

"So was I, Horry. I laughed at him. I'd give anything not to have."

"You didn't matter...."

He was silent a moment. Then he swung round, full to her. His face burned, his eyes flashed tears; he held his head up to stop them falling.

"Barbara—if he dies, I'll kill myself."

That evening Mr. Waddington's temperature went up another point. Ralph, calling about nine o'clock, found Barbara alone in the library, huddled in a corner of the sofa, with her pocket-handkerchief beside her, rolled in a tight, damp ball. She started as he came in.

"Oh," she said, "I thought you were the doctor."

"Do you want him?"

"Yes. Fanny does. She's frightened."

"Shall I go and get him?"

"No. No. They've sent Kimber. Oh, Ralph, I'm frightened, too."

"But he's getting on all right. He is really. Ransome says so."

"I know. I've told them that. But they won't believe it. And I don't now. He'll die: you'll see he'll die. Just because we've been such pigs to him."

"Nonsense; that wouldn't make him—"

"I'm not so sure. It's awful to see him lying there, like a lamb—so good— when you think how we've hunted and hounded him."

"He didn't know, Barbara. We never let him know."

"You don't know what he knew. He must have seen it."

"He never sees anything."

"I tell you, you don't know what he sees.... I'd give anything, anything not to have done it."

"So would I."

"It's a lesson to me," she said, "as long as I live, never to laugh at anybody again. Never to say cruel things."

"We didn't say cruel things."

"Unkind things."

"Not very unkind."

"We did. I did. I said all the really beastly ones."

"No. No, you didn't. Not half as beastly as I and Horry did."

"That's what Horry's thinking now. He's nearly off his head about it."

"Look here, Barbara; you're simply sentimentalizing because he's ill and you're sorry for him.... You needn't be. I tell you, he's enjoying his illness. ... I don't suppose," said Ralph thoughtfully, "he's enjoyed anything so much since the war."

"Doesn't that show what brutes we've been, that he has to be ill in order to enjoy himself?"

"Oh, no. He enjoys himself—himself, Barbara—all the time. He can't help enjoying his illness. He likes to have everybody fussing round him and thinking about him."

"That's what I mean. We never did think of him. Not seriously. We've done nothing—nothing but laugh. Why, you're laughing now. ... It's horrible of you, Ralph, when he may be dying. ... It would serve us all jolly well right if he did die."

To her surprise and indignation, Barbara began to cry. The hard, damp lump of pocket-handkerchief was not a bit of good, and before she could reach out for it Ralph's arms were round her and he was kissing the tears off one by one.

"Darling, I didn't think you really minded—"

"What d-did you th-think, then?" she sobbed.

"I thought you were playing. A sort of variation of the game."

"I told you it was a cruel game."

"Never mind. It's all over. We'll never play it again. And he'll be well in another week. ... Look here, Barbara, can't you leave off thinking about him for a minute? You know I love you, most awfully, don't you?"

"Yes. I know now all right."

"And *I* know."

"How do you know?"

"Because, old thing, you've never ceased to hang on to my collar since I grabbed you. You can't go back on *that.*"

"I don't want to go back on it.... I say, we always said he brought us together, and he *has*, this time."

When later that night Ralph told Fanny of their engagement the first thing she said was, "You mustn't tell him. Not till he's well again. In fact, I'd rather you didn't tell him till just before you're married."

"Why ever not?"

"It might upset him. You see," she said, "he's very fond of Barbara."

The next day Mr. Waddington's temperature went down to normal; and the next, when Ralph called, Barbara fairly rushed at him with the news.

"He's sitting up," she shouted, "eating a piece of sole."

"Hooray! Now we can be happy."

The sound of Fanny's humming came through the drawing-room door.

XV

1

Mr. Waddington was sitting up in his armchair before the bedroom fire. By turning his head a little to the right he could command a perfect view of himself in the long glass by the window. To get up and look at himself in that glass had been the first act of his convalescence. He had hardly dared to think what alterations his illness might have made in him. He remembered the horrible sight that Corbett had presented after *his* influenza last year.

Looking earnestly at himself in the glass, he had found that his appearance was, if anything, improved. Outlines that he had missed for the last ten years were showing up again. The Postlethwaite nose was cleaner cut. He was almost slender, and not half so weak as Fanny said he ought to have been. Immobility in bed, his spiritual attitude of complacent acquiescence, and the release of his whole organism from the strain of a restless intellect had set him up more than his influenza had pulled him down; and it was a distinctly more refined and youthful Waddington that Barbara found sitting in the armchair, wearing a royal blue wadded silk dressing-gown and Fanny's motor-scarf, with a grey mohair shawl over his knees.

Mr. Waddington's convalescence was altogether delightful to him, admitting, as it did, of sustained companionship with Barbara. As soon as it reached the armchair stage she sat with him for hours together. She had finished the Ramblings, and at his request she read them aloud to him all over again from beginning to end. Mr. Waddington was much gratified by the impression they made recited in Barbara's charming voice; the voice that trembled a little now and then with an emotion that did her credit.

"'Come with me into the little sheltered valley of the Speed. Let us follow the brown trout stream that goes purling through the lush green grass of the meadows—'"

"I'd no idea," said Mr. Waddington, "it was anything like so good as it is. We may congratulate ourselves on having got rid of Ralph Bevan."

And in February, when the frost broke and the spring weather came, and the green and pink and purple fields showed up again through the mist on the hillsides, he went out driving with Barbara in his car. He wanted to look again at the places of his *Ramblings*, and he wanted Barbara to look at them with him. It was the reward he had promised her for what he called her dreary, mechanical job of copying and copying.

Barbara noticed the curious, exalted expression of his face as he sat up beside her in the car, looking noble. She put it down partly to that everlasting self-satisfaction that made his inward happiness, and partly to sheer physical exhilaration induced by speed. She felt something like it herself as they tore switchbacking up and down the hills: an excitement whipped up on the top of the deep happiness that came from thinking about Ralph. And there was hardly a moment when she didn't think about him. It made her eyes shine and her mouth quiver with a peculiarly blissful smile.

And Mr. Waddington looked at Barbara where she sat tucked up beside him. He noticed the shining and the quivering, and he thought—what he always had thought of Barbara. Only now he was certain.

The child loved him. She had been fascinated and frightened, frightened and fascinated by him from the first hour that she had known him. But she was not afraid of him any more. She had left off struggling. She was giving herself up like a child to this feeling, the nature of which, in her child's innocence, she did not yet know. But he knew. He had always known it.

So much one half of Mr. Waddington's mind admitted, while the other half denied that he had known it with any certainty. It went on saying to itself: "Blind. Blind. Yet I might have known it," as if he hadn't.

He had, of course, kept it before him as a possibility (no part of him denied that). And he had used tact. He had handled a delicate situation with a consummate delicacy. He had done everything an honourable man could do. But there it was. There it had been from the day that he had come into the house and found her there. And the thing was too strong for Barbara. Poor child, he might have known it would be. And it was too strong for Mr. Waddington. It wasn't his fault. It was Fanny's fault, having the girl there and forcing them to that dangerous intimacy.

Before his illness Mr. Waddington had resisted successfully any little inclination he might have had to take advantage of the situation. He conceived his inner life for the last nine months as consisting of a series of resistances. He conceived the episode of Elise as a safety valve, natural but unpleasant, for the emotions caused by Barbara: the substitution of a permissible for an impermissible lapse. It had been incredible to him that he should make love to Barbara.

But one effect of his influenza was apparent. It had lowered his resistance, and, lowering it, had altered his whole moral perspective and his scale of values, till one morning in April, walking with Barbara in the garden that smelt of wallflowers and violets, he became aware that Barbara was as necessary to him as he was to Barbara.

Her easel stood in a corner of the lawn with an unfinished water-colour drawing of the house on it. He paused before it, smiling his tender, sentimental smile.

"There's one thing I regret, Barbara—that I didn't have your drawings for my Cotswold book."

The *Ramblings*, thanks to unproclaimed activities of Ralph Bevan, were at that moment in the press.

"Why should you," she said, "if you didn't care about them?"

"It's inconceivable that I shouldn't have cared. ... I was blind. Blind. ... Well, some day, if we ever have an *édition de luxe*, they shall appear in that."

"Some day!"

She hadn't the heart to tell him that the drawings had another destination, for as yet the existence of Ralph's took was a secret. They had agreed that nothing should disturb Mr. Waddington's pleasure in the publication of his Ramblings—his poor Ramblings.

"One has to pay for blindness in this world," he said.

"A lot of people'll be let in at that rate. I don't suppose five will care a rap about my drawings."

"I wasn't thinking only of your drawings, my dear." He pondered. ... "Fanny tells me you're going to have a birthday. You're quite a little April girl, aren't you?"

2

It was Barbara's twenty-fourth birthday, and the day of her adoption. It had begun, unpropitiously, with something very like a dispute between Horatio and Fanny.

Mr. Waddington had gone up to London the day before, and had returned with a pearl pendant for Fanny, and a green jade necklace for Barbara (not yet presented) and a canary yellow waistcoat for himself.

And not only the waistcoat—

On the birthday morning Fanny had called out to Barbara as she passed her bedroom door:

"Barbara, come here."

Fanny was staring, fascinated, at four pairs of silk pyjamas spread out before her on the bed. Remarkable pyjamas, of a fierce magenta with forked lightning in orange running about all over them.

"Good God, Fanny!"

"You may well say 'Good God.' What would you say if you'd got to...? I'm not a nervous woman, but—"

"It's a mercy he didn't get them eighteen years ago," said Barbara, "or Horry might have been born an idiot."

"Yellow waistcoats are all very well," said Fanny. "But what *can* he have been thinking of?"

"I don't know," said Barbara. Somehow the pattern called up, irresistibly, the image of Mrs. Levitt.

"Perhaps," she said, "he thinks he's Jupiter."

"Well, I'm not What's-her-name, and I don't want to be blasted. So I'll put them somewhere where he can't find them."

At that moment they had heard Mr. Waddington coming through his dressing-room and Barbara had run away by the door into the corridor.

"Who took those things out of my wardrobe?" he said. He was gazing, dreamily, affectionately almost, at the pyjamas.

"I did."

"And what for?"

"To look at them. Can you wonder? Horatio, if you wear them I'll apply for a separation."

"You needn't worry."

There was a queer look in his face, significant and furtive. And Fanny's mind, with one of its rapid flights, darted off from the pyjamas.

"What are you going to do about Barbara?" she said.

"*Do* about her?"

"Yes. You know we were going to adopt her if we liked her enough. And we do like her enough, don't we?"

"I have no paternal feeling for Barbara," said Mr. Waddington. "The parental relation does not appeal to me as desirable or suitable."

"I should have thought, considering her age and your age, it was very suitable indeed."

"Not if it entails obligations that I might regret."

"You're going to provide for her, aren't you? That isn't an obligation, surely, you'll regret?"

"I can provide for her without adopting her."

"How? It's no good just leaving her something in your will."

"I shall continue half her salary," said Mr. Waddington, "as an allowance."

"Yes. But will you give her a marriage portion if she marries?"

He was silent. His mind reeled with the blow.

"If she marries," he said, "with my consent and my approval—yes."

"If that isn't a parental attitude! And supposing she doesn't?"

"She isn't thinking of marrying."

"You don't know what she's thinking of."

"Neither, I venture to say, do you."

"Well—I don't see how I can adopt her, if you don't."

"I didn't say I wouldn't adopt her."

"Then you will?"

He snapped back at her with an incredible ferocity.

"I suppose I shall have to. Don't *worry* me!"

He then lifted up the pyjamas from the bed and carried them into his dressing-room. Through the open door she saw him, mounted on a chair, laying them out, tenderly, on the top shelf of the wardrobe: as if he were storing them for some mysterious and romantic purpose in which Fanny was not included.

"Perhaps, after all," she thought, "he only bought them because they make him feel young."

All the morning, that morning of Barbara's birthday and adoption Mr. Waddington's thoughtful gloom continued. And in the afternoon he shut himself up in his library and gave orders that he was not to be disturbed.

3

Barbara was in the morning-room.

They had given her the morning-room for a study, and she was alone in it, amusing herself with her pocket sketch-book.

The sketch-book was Barbara's and Ralph's secret. Sometimes it lived for days with Ralph at the White Hart. Sometimes it lived with Barbara, in her coat pocket, or in her bureau under lock and key. She was obsessed with the fear that some day she would leave it about and Fanny would find it, or Mr. Waddington. Or any minute Mr. Waddington might come on her and catch her with it. It would be awful if she were caught. For that remarkable collection contained several pen-and-ink drawings of Mr. Waddington, and Barbara added to their number daily.

But at the moment, the long interval between an unusually early birthday tea and an unusually late birthday dinner, she was safe. Fanny had gone over to Medlicott in the car. Mr. Waddington was tucked away in his library, reading in perfect innocence and simplicity and peace. It wasn't even likely that Ralph would turn up, for he had gone over to Oxford, and it was on his account that the birthday dinner was put off till half-past eight. There would be hours and hours.

She had just finished the last of three drawings of Mr. Waddington: Mr. Waddington standing up before the long looking-glass in his new pyjamas; Mr. Waddington appearing in the doorway of Fanny's bedroom as Jupiter, with forked lightning zig-zagging out of him into every corner; Mr. Waddington stooping to climb into his bed, a broad back view with lightnings blazing out of it.

And it was that moment that Mr. Waddington chose to come in to present the green jade necklace. He was wearing his canary yellow waistcoat.

Barbara closed her sketch-book hurriedly and laid it on the table. She kept one arm over it while she received and opened the leather case where the green necklace lay on its white cushion.

"For *me*? Oh, it's too heavenly. How awfully sweet of you."

"Do you like it, Barbara?"

"I love it."

Compunction stung her when she thought of her drawings, especially the one where he was getting into bed. She said to herself: "I'll never do it again. Never again…. And I won't show it to Ralph."

"Put it on," he commanded, "and let me see you in it."

She lifted it from the case. She raised her arms and clasped it round her neck; she went to the looking-glass. And, after the first rapt moment of admiration, Mr. Waddington possessed himself of the uncovered sketch-book. Barbara saw him in the looking-glass. She turned, with a cry:

"You mustn't! You mustn't look at it."

"Why not?"

"Because I don't let anybody see my sketches."

"You'll let *me*."

"I *won't!*" She dashed at him, clutching his arm and hanging her weight on it. He shook himself free and raised the sketch-book high above her head. She jumped up, tearing at it, but his grip held.

He delighted in his power. He laughed.

"Give it me this instant," she said.

"Aha! She's got her little secrets, has she?"

"Yes. Yes. They're all there. You've no business to look at them."

He caracoled heavily, dodging her attack, enjoying the youthful violence of the struggle.

"Come," he said, "ask me nicely."

"Please, then. *Please* give it me."

He gave it, bowing profoundly over her hand as she took it.

"I wouldn't look into your dear little secrets for the world," he said.

They sat down amicably.

"You'll let me stay with you a little while?"

"Please do. Won't you have one of my cigarettes?"

He took one, turning it in his fingers and smiling at it—a lingering, sentimental smile.

"I think I know your secret," he said presently.

"Do you?" Her mind rushed to Ralph.

"I think so. And I think you know mine."

"Yours?"

"Yes. Mine. We can't go on living like this, so close to each other, without knowing. We may try to keep things from each other, but we can't. I feel as if you'd seen everything."

She said to herself: "He's thinking of Mrs. Levitt."

"I don't suppose I've seen anything that matters," she said.

"You've seen what my life is here. You can't have helped seeing that Fanny and I don't hit it off very well together."

"Fanny's an angel."

"You dear little loyal thing.... Yes, she's an angel. Too much of an angel for a mere man. I made my grand mistake, Barbara, when I married her."

"She doesn't think so, anyhow."

"I'm not so sure. Fanny knows she's got hold of something that's too—too big for her. What's wrong with Fanny is that she can't grasp things. She's afraid of them. And she can't take serious things seriously. It's no use expecting her to. I've left off expecting."

"You don't understand Fanny one bit."

"My dear child, I've been married to her more than seventeen years, and I'm not a fool. You've seen for yourself how she takes things. How she belittles everything with her everlasting laugh, laugh, laugh. In time it gets on your nerves."

"It would," said Barbara, "if you don't see the fun of it."

"You can't expect me to see the fun of my own funeral."

"Funeral? Is it as bad as all that?"

"It has been as bad as all that—Barbara."

He brooded.

"And then you came, with your sweetness. And your little serious face—"

"*Is* my face serious?"

"Very. To me. Other people may think you frivolous and amusing. I daresay you are amusing—to them."

"I hope so."

"You hope so because you want to hide your real self from them. But you can't hide it from me. I've seen it all the time, Barbara."

"Are you sure?"

"Quite, quite sure."

"I wish I knew what it looked like."

"That's the beauty and charm of you, my dear, that you don't know."

"What a nice waistcoat you've got on," said Barbara.

He looked gratified. "I'm glad you like it I put it on for your birthday."

"You mean," she said, "my adoption day."

He winced.

"It *is* good," she said, "of you and Fanny to adopt me. But it won't be for very long. And I want to earn my own living all the same."

"I can't think of letting you do that."

"I must. It won't make any difference to my adoption."

He scowled. So repugnant to him was this subject that he judged it would be equally distasteful to Barbara.

"It was Fanny's idea," he said.

"I thought it would be."

"You didn't expect me to have paternal feelings for you, Barbara?"

"I didn't *expect* you to have any feelings at all."

The wound made him start. "My poor child, what a terrible thing for you to say."

"Why terrible?"

"Because it shows—it shows—And it isn't true. Do you suppose I don't know what's been going on inside you? I was blind to myself, my dear, but I saw through you."

"Saw through me?" She thought again of Ralph.

"Through and through."

"I didn't know I was so transparent. But I don't see that it matters much if you did."

He smiled at her delicious naivete.

"No. Nothing matters. Nothing matters, Barbara, except our caring. At least we're wise enough to know that."

"I shouldn't have thought," she said, "it would take much wisdom."

"More than you think, my child; more than you think. You've only got to be wise for yourself. I've got to be wise for both of us."

She thought: "Heavy parent. That comes of being adopted."

"When it comes to the point," she said, "one can only be wise for oneself."

"I'm glad you see that. It makes it much easier for me."

"It does. You mustn't think you're responsible for me just because you've adopted me."

"Don't talk to me about adoption! When you know perfectly well what I did it for."

"Why—what *did* you do it for?"

"To make things safe for us. To keep Fanny from knowing. To keep myself from knowing, Barbara. To keep you.... But it's too late to camouflage it. We know where we stand now."

"I don't think *I* do."

"You do. You do."

Mr. Waddington tossed his cigarette into the fire with a passionate gesture of abandonment. He came to her. She saw his coming. She saw it chiefly as the approach of a canary yellow waistcoat. She fixed her attention on the waistcoat as if it were the centre of her own mental equilibrium.

There was a bend in the waistcoat. Mr. Waddington was stooping over her with his face peering into hers. She sat motionless, held under his face by curiosity and fear. The whole phenomenon seemed to her incredible. Too incredible as yet to call for protest. It was as if it were not happening; as if she were merely waiting to see it happen before she cried out. Yet she was frightened.

This state lasted for one instant. The next she was in his arms. His mouth, thrust out under the big, rough moustache, was running over her face, like— like—while she pressed her hands hard against the canary yellow waistcoat, pushing him off, her mind disengaged itself from the struggle and reported— like a vacuum cleaner. That was it. Vacuum cleaner.

He gave back. There was no evil violence in him, and she got on her feet.

"How could you?" she cried. "How could you be such a perfect pig?"

"*Don't* say that to me, Barbara. Even in fun.... You know you love me."

"I don't. I don't."

"You do. You know you do. You know you want me to take you in my arms. Why be so cruel to yourself?"

"To myself? I'd kill myself before I let you.... Why, I'd kill you."

"No. No. No. You only think you would, you little spitfire."

He had given back altogether and now leaned against the chimneypiece, not beaten, not abashed, but smiling at her in a triumphant certitude. For so long the glamour of his illusion held him.

"Nothing you can say, Barbara, will persuade me that you don't care for me."

"Then you must be mad. Mad as a hatter."

"All men go mad at times. You must make allowances. Listen—"

"I won't listen. I don't want to hear another word."

She was going.

He saw her intention; but he was nearer to the door than she was, and by a quick though ponderous movement he got there first. He stood before her with his back to the door. (He had the wild thought of locking it, but chivalry forbade him.)

"You can go in a minute," he said. "But you've got to listen to me first. You've got to be fair to me. I may be mad; but if I didn't care for you—madly—I wouldn't have supposed for an instant that you cared for me. I wouldn't have thought of such a thing."

"But I *don't*, I tell you."

"And I tell you, you do. Do you suppose after all you've done for me—"

"I haven't done anything."

"Done? Look at the way you've worked for me. I've never known anything like your devotion, Barbara."

"Oh, *that*! It was only my job."

"Was it your job to save me from that horrible woman?"

"Oh, yes; it was all in the day's work."

"My dear Barbara, no woman ever does a day's work like that for a man unless she cares for him. And unless she wants him to care for her."

"As it happens, it was Fanny I cared for. I was thinking of Fanny all the time…. If *you'd* think about Fanny more and about Mrs. Levitt and people less, it would be a good thing."

"It's too late to think about Fanny now. That's only your sweetness and goodness."

"Please don't lie. If you really thought me sweet and good you wouldn't expect me to be a substitute for Mrs. Levitt."

"Don't talk about Mrs. Levitt. Do you suppose I think of you in the same sentence? That was a different thing altogether."

"Was it? Was it so very different?"

He saw that she remembered. "It was. A man may lose his head ten times over without losing his heart once. If it's Mrs. Levitt you're thinking about, you can put that out of your mind for ever."

"It isn't only Mrs. Levitt. There's Ralph Bevan. You've forgotten Ralph Bevan."

"What has Ralph Bevan got to do with it?"

"Simply this, that I'm engaged to be married to him."

"To be married? To be married to Ralph Bevan? Oh, Barbara, why didn't you tell me?"

"Ralph didn't want me to, till nearer the time."

"The time…. Did it come to that?"

"It did," said Barbara.

He moved from the doorway and began walking up and down the room. She might now have gone out, but she didn't go. She *had* to see what he would make of it.

At his last turn he faced her and stood still.

"Poor child," he said, "so that's what I've driven you to?"

Amazement kept her silent.

"Sit down," he said, "we must go through this together."

Amazement made her sit down. Certainly they must go through it, to see what he would look like at the end. He was unsurpassable. She mustn't miss him.

"Look here, Barbara." He spoke in a tone of forced, unnatural calm. "I don't think you quite understand the situation. I'm sure you don't realize for one moment how serious it is."

"I don't. You mustn't expect me to take it seriously."

"That's because you don't take yourself seriously enough, dear. In some ways you're singularly humble. I don't believe you really know how deep this thing has gone with me, or you wouldn't have talked about Mrs. Levitt.…

"… It's life and death, Barbara. Life and death…. I'll make a confession. It wasn't serious at first. It wasn't love at first sight. But it's gone all the deeper for that. I didn't know how deep it was till the other day. And I had so much to think of. So many claims. Fanny—"

"Yes. Don't forget Fanny."

"I am not forgetting her. Fanny isn't going to mind as you think she minds. As you would mind yourself if you were in her place. Things don't go so deep with Fanny as all that…. And she isn't going to hold me against my will. She's not that sort…. Listen, now. Please listen."

Barbara sat still, listening. She would let him go to the end of his tether.

"I'll confess. In the beginning I hadn't thought of a divorce. I couldn't bear the idea of going through all that unpleasantness. But I'd go through it ten times over rather than that you should marry Ralph Bevan.... Wait now.... Before I spoke to you to-day I'd made up my mind to ask Fanny to divorce me. I know she'll do it. Your name shan't be allowed to appear. The moment I get her consent we'll go off together somewhere. Italy or the Riviera. I've got everything planned, everything ready. I saw to that when I was in London. I've bought everything—"

She saw forked lightnings on a magenta Waddington.

"What are you laughing at, Barbara?"

He stood over her, distressed. Was *Barbara* going to treat him to a fit of hysterics?

"Don't laugh. Don't be silly, child."

But Barbara went on laughing, with her face in the cushions, abandoned to her vision. From far up the park they heard the sound of Kimber's hooter, then the grinding of the car, with Fanny in it, on the gravel outside. Barbara sat up suddenly and dried her eyes.

They stared at each other, the stare of accomplices.

"Come, child," he said, "pull yourself together."

Barbara got up and looked in the glass and saw the green jade necklace hanging on her still. She took it off and laid it on the table beside the forgotten sketch-book.

"I think," she said, "you must have meant this for Mrs. Levitt. But you may thank your stars it's only me, this time."

He pretended not to hear her, not to see the necklace, not to know that she was going from him. She stood a moment with her back to the door, facing him. It was her turn to stand there and be listened to.

"Mr. Waddington," she said, "some people might think you wicked. I only think you funny."

He drew himself up and looked noble.

"Funny? If that's your idea of me, you had better marry Ralph Bevan."

"I almost think I had."

And she laughed again. Not Mrs. Levitt's laughter, gross with experience. He had borne that without much pain. Girl's laughter it was, young and innocent and pure, and ten times more cruel.

"You don't know," she said, "you don't know how funny you are," and left him.

Mr. Waddington took up the necklace and kissed it. He rubbed it against his cheek and kissed it. A slip of paper had fallen from the table to the floor. He knew what was written on it: "From Horatio Bysshe Waddington to his Little April Girl." He took it up and put it in his pocket. He took up the sketch-book.

"The little thing," he thought. "Now, if it hadn't been for her ridiculous jealousy of Elise—if it hadn't been for Fanny—if it hadn't been for the little thing's sweetness and goodness—" Her goodness. She was a saint. A saint. It was Barbara's virtue, not Barbara, that had repulsed him.

This was the only credible explanation of her behaviour, the only one he could bear to live with.

He opened the sketch-book.

It was Fanny, coming in that instant, who saved him from the worst.

When she had restored the sketch-book to its refuge in the bureau and locked it in, she turned to him.

"Horatio," she said, "as Ralph's coming to dinner to-night I'd better tell you that he and Barbara are engaged to be married."

"She has told me herself…. That child, Fanny, is a saint. A little saint."

"How did you find that out? Do you think it takes a saint to marry Ralph?"

"I think it takes a saint to—to marry Ralph, since you put it that way."

4

"Dearest Fanny:

"I'm sorry, but Mr. Waddington and I have had a scrap. It's made things impossible, and I'm going to Ralph. He'll turn out for me, so there won't be any scandal.

"You know how awfully I love you, that's why you'll forgive me if I don't come back.

"Always your loving

"Barbara."

"P.S.—I'm frightfully sorry about my birthday dinner. But I don't feel birthdayish or dinnerish, either. I want Ralph. Nothing but Ralph."

That would make Fanny think it was Ralph they had quarrelled about. Barbara put this note on Fanny's dressing-table. Then she went up to the White Hart, to Ralph Bevan. She waited in his sitting-room till he came back from Oxford.

"Hallo, old thing, what are *you* doing here?"

"Ralph—do you awfully mind if we don't dine at the Manor?"

"If we don't—why?"

"Because I've left them. And I don't want to go back. Do you think I could get a room here?"

"What's up?"

"I've had a simply awful scrap with Waddy, and I can't stick it there. Between us we've made it impossible."

"What's he been up to?"

"Oh, never mind."

"He's been making love to you."

"If you call it making love."

"The old swine!"

As he said it, he felt the words and his own fury fall short of the fantastic quality of Waddington.

"No. He isn't." (Barbara felt it.) "He was simply more funny than you can imagine.... He had on a canary yellow waistcoat."

In spite of his fury he smiled.

"I think he'd bought it for that."

"Oh, Barbara, what he must have looked like!"

"Yes. If only you could have seen him. But that's the worst of all his best things. They only happen when you're alone with him."

"You remember—we wondered whether he'd do it again, whether he'd go one better?"

"Yes, Ralph. We little thought it would be me."

"How he does surpass himself!"

"The funniest thing was he thought I was in love with *him*."

"He didn't!"

"He did. Because of the way I'd worked for him. He thought that proved it."

"Yes. Yes. I suppose he *would* think it.... Look here—he didn't do anything, did he?"

"He kissed me. *That* wasn't funny."

"The putrid old sinner. If he *wasn't* so old I'd wring his neck for him."

"No, no. That's all wrong. It's not the way we agreed to take him. We'd think it funny enough if he'd done it to somebody else. It's pure accident that it's me."

"No doubt that's the proper philosophic view. I wonder whether Mrs. Levitt takes it."

"Ralph—it wasn't a bit like his Mrs. Levitt stunt. The awful thing was he really meant it. He'd planned it all out. We were to go off together to the Riviera, and he was to wear his canary waistcoat."

"Did he say that?"

"No. But you could see he thought it. And he was going to get Fanny to divorce him."

"Good God! He went as far as that?"

"As far as that. He was so cocksure, you see. I'm afraid it's been a bit of a shock to him."

"Well, it's a thundering good thing I've got a job at last."

"*Have* you?"

"Yes. We can get married the day after tomorrow if we like. Blackadder's given me the editorship of the *New Review*."

"No? Oh, Ralph, how topping."

"That's what I ran up to Oxford for, to see him and settle everything. It's a fairly decent screw. The thing's got no end of hacking, and it's up to me to make it last."

"I say—Fanny'll he pleased."

As they were talking about it, the landlady of the White Hart came in to tell them that Mrs. Waddington was downstairs and wanted to speak to Miss Madden.

"All right," Ralph said. "Show Mrs. Waddington up. I'll clear out."

"Oh, Ralph, what am I to say to her?"

"Tell her the truth, if she wants it. She won't mind."

"She will—frightfully."

"Not so frightfully as you think."

"That's what *he* said."

"Well, he's right there, the old beast."

5

"Barbara *dear*," said Fanny when they were alone together, "what on earth has happened?"

"Oh, nothing. We just had a bit of a tiff, that's all."

"About Ralph? He told me it was Ralph."

"You might say it was Ralph. He came into it."

"Into what?"

"Oh, the general situation."

"Nonsense. Horatio was making love to you. I could see by his face.... You needn't mind telling me straight out I've seen it coming."

"Since when?"

"I don't know. It must have begun long before I saw it."

"How long do you think?"

"Oh, before Mrs. Levitt."

"Mrs. Levitt?"

"She may have been only a safety valve. That's why I made him adopt you. I thought it would stop it. In common decency. But it seems it only brought it to a head."

"No. It was his canary waistcoat did that, Fanny."

The ghost of dead mirth rose up in Fanny's eyes.

"You're muddling cause and effect, my dear. He wasn't in love because he bought the waistcoat. He bought the waistcoat because he was in love. And those other things—the romantic pyjamas—because he thought they'd make him look younger."

"Well then," said Barbara, "it was a vicious circle. The waistcoat put it into his head that afternoon."

"It doesn't much matter how it happened."

"I'm awfully sorry, Fanny. I wouldn't have let it happen for the world, if I'd known it was going to. But who could have known?"

"My dear, it wasn't your fault."

"Do you mind frightfully?"

Fanny looked away.

"It depends," she said. "What did you say to him?"

"I said a lot of things, but they weren't a bit of good. Then I'm afraid I laughed."

"You laughed at him?"

"I couldn't help it, Fanny. He was so funny."

"Oh!" Fanny caught her breath back on a sob. "That's what I can't bear, Barbara—his being laughed at."

"I know," said Barbara.

"By the way, when you're dying dear, if you should be dying at any time, it'll be a consolation to you to know that he didn't see your drawings—"

"Did *you* see them?"

"Only the one he was looking at when I came in."

"Was it—was it the one where he was getting into bed?"

"No. He was only hunting."

"God has been kinder to me than I deserve then."

"He's been kinder to him, too, I fancy."

She went on. "I want you to see this thing straight. Understand. I don't mind his being in love with you. I knew he was. Head over ears in love. And I didn't mind a bit."

"I think he was reckoning on that. He knew you'd forgive him."

"Forgive him? It wasn't even a question of forgiveness. I was *glad*. I thought: If only he could have one real feeling. If only he could care for something or somebody that wasn't himself.... I think he cared for you, Barbara. It wasn't just himself. And I loved him for it."

"You darling! And you don't hate me?"

"You know I don't But I'd love you even more if you'd loved him."

"If I'd loved him?"

"Yes. If you'd gone away with him and made him happy. If you hadn't laughed at him, Barbara."

"I know. It was awful of me. But what could I do?"

"What could you do? We all do it. I do it. Mrs. Levitt did it."

"I didn't do it like Mrs. Levitt."

"No. But you were just one more. Think of it. All his life to be laughed at. And when he was making love, too; the most serious thing, Barbara, that anybody can do. I tell you I can't bear it. I'd have given him to you ten times first."

"Then," said Barbara, "you *have* got to forgive me."

"If I don't, it's because it's my own sin and I can't forgive myself...."

"... Besides, I let it happen. Because I thought it would cure him."

"Of falling in love?"

"Of trying to be young when he didn't feel it. I thought he'd see how impossible it was. But that's the sad part of it. He *would* have felt young, Barbara, if you'd loved him. If I'd loved him I could have kept him young. I told you," she said, "it was all my fault."

"You told me Ralph and I would never be old. Is that what you meant?"

"Yes."

They sat silent a moment, looking down through Ralph's window into the Market Square.

And presently they saw Mr. Waddington pass the corner of the Town Hall and cross the wide, open space to the Dower House.

"You must come back with me, Barbara. If you don't everybody'll know what's happened."

"I can't, Fanny."

"He won't be there. You won't see him till your wedding day. He's going to stay with Granny. He says she isn't very well."

"I'm sorry she isn't well."

"She's perfectly well. That isn't what he's going for."

Across the Square they could see the door of the Dower House open and receive him. Fanny smiled.

"He's going back to his mother to be made young again," she said.